KILLER CHATGPT™ PROMPTS

Harness the Power of AI for Success and Profit

T0049695

GUY HART-DAVIS

WILEY

Contents

Introduction

CHATGPT IS THE hottest technology around as of this writing. A huge number of companies and organizations are using ChatGPT in the workplace. So are government bodies. Students, teachers, and administrators are using ChatGPT at all levels of education, from kindergarten through to postgraduate and doctoral. Entrepreneurs are using ChatGPT to turbocharge their productivity and create new products without raising their staffing costs. Even the military is using Chat-GPT, both in the workplace and in the field (don't ask).

But what *is* ChatGPT?

What Is ChatGPT?

ChatGPT is an artificial intelligence tool created by the OpenAI research laboratory. OpenAI consists of two parts: a nonprofit organization called OpenAI Incorporated, and its for-profit subsidiary corporation, OpenAI Limited Partnership. OpenAI was founded in 2015 and is based in San Francisco, CA. OpenAI launched ChatGPT on November 30, 2022.

What does the name ChatGPT mean? Well, *GPT* is the abbreviation for Generative Pre-trained Transformer. Here's what each of those words means:

- **Generative:** GPT generates text.
- **Pre-trained:** OpenAI has trained GPT on a vast body of text — not actually everything on the web, but huge chunks of what's available there.
- **Transformer:** In machine learning, a *transformer* is a deep learning model that can give different weight (significance) to different parts of the input. For example, when you feed a sentence into a transformer, it gives the different words and phrases different significance rather than treating them all as equally important. Transformers are used mostly in natural language processing (NLP) and computer vision (CV).

GPT is what's called a "large language model." Briefly, a *language model* is a probability distribution over a given piece of text — a mathematical function that describes how probable it is that a particular word will occur. A *large language model* is simply a language model that uses a large amount of text.

That's GPT. *Chat* just means talking in an informal way, as usual. Thus, ChatGPT is a chatbot, a robot (or bot) designed for chatting.

What Can ChatGPT Do for You?

"Chatting" may sound trivial, but ChatGPT can do a huge amount for you — everything from streamlining your work at the office through to supporting your studies and giving you tips for running your home more efficiently.

Here's a taste of what you'll learn to do with ChatGPT in this book:

- Create a ChatGPT account and set up ChatGPT on your desktop, laptop, smartphone, or tablet (Chapter 1).
- Optimize your resume and turbocharge your job hunt (Chapter 2).

- Streamline meetings and manage your email (Chapter 3).
- Create business documents and have ChatGPT edit and proof-read your work (Chapter 4).
- Research topics in depth, analyze data, and gain business insights (Chapter 5).
- Improve your company's communications and knowledge sharing (Chapter 6).
- Assess competitive websites and create HTML, CSS, and scripts for your website (Chapter 7).
- Write programming code — and debug, optimize, and refactor it (Chapter 8).
- Draft job descriptions and job ads, develop onboarding and training materials, and gather employee feedback (Chapter 9).
- Create marketing content, develop sales materials, and engage customers via email (Chapter 10).
- Write a course description, course goals, and course objectives for a course you'll teach; develop lesson plans, reading lists, and activities; and create tests (Chapter 11).
- Boost your studies by enlisting ChatGPT's help to practice languages, finish your homework, kick-start your writing assignments, and create practice tests (Chapter 12).
- Blast through writer's block and generate plots, characters, and dialogue (Chapter 13).
- Streamline and automate home tasks from the kitchen to the garden, and improve your entertainment (Chapter 14).
- Gather advice on anything from medical problems to relationships and your finances (Chapter 15).

How Do You Get Started?

To get started with ChatGPT, set up an account with OpenAI — either a free account or a paid account. You can then access ChatGPT through a web browser on any device. To use ChatGPT on an iPhone or iPad, install the official ChatGPT app from the App Store.

Similarly, to use ChatGPT on an Android device, install the official ChatGPT app from the Play Store. Chapter 1 gives you the details on all of this.

Once you're signed in to the service, you tell ChatGPT what you want it to do. These instructions are called *prompts*. This book shows you how to prompt ChatGPT effectively.

Turn the page, and we'll begin.

1

Get Started with ChatGPT Prompts

In this chapter, you set yourself up to use ChatGPT and learn the essentials of giving prompts. I suggest you begin by setting up a free research preview account so that you can take ChatGPT for a spin without having to pay. You can then start prompting ChatGPT for information and evaluate the responses it returns.

Assuming you like what you see, you can upgrade from the free account to a paid account, which gives you access to the full range of ChatGPT's features.

Whether you go for a paid account or stick with the free preview account, you can choose settings to control how the account works. The paid account has a few more settings, which we'll cover in this chapter, too.

Toward the end of the chapter, we'll look at how to set up Chat-GPT on your other computers and on your iPhone, iPad, or Android device.

Set Up a Free Research Preview Account

If you want to test ChatGPT before you start paying for it, set up a free account. A free account enables you to use enough of ChatGPT's features to evaluate it effectively. You don't get access to the latest and most advanced features, and ChatGPT may respond more slowly when the service is busy, because it gives priority to its paying customers.

Setting up an account takes only a couple of minutes, so there's no downside. You need to provide an email address, which OpenAI uses as the ID for your account, and a phone number, which OpenAI uses for verification.

NOTE   As well as letting you create a research preview account using your email address, the Create Your Account screen enables you to create your account by using your Google Account, your Microsoft Account, or your Apple ID. Click the Continue with Google button, the Continue with Microsoft Account button, or the Continue with Apple button if you want to use one of these options.

To set up your research preview account, open a web browser to chat.openai.com, click the Sign Up button to display the Create Your Account screen (see Figure 1-1), and then follow the prompts. These are the key steps:

1. To verify your email address, OpenAI sends you an email, which you may need to retrieve from your Junk folder; click the Verify Email Address button to perform the verification.

2. On the Tell Us About You screen, enter your first name, last name, and birthday (to verify you're old enough to use Chat-GPT), and click another Continue button.

3. On the Verify Your Phone Number screen, pick your country from the drop-down list, type your phone number, and then click the Send Code button. When your phone receives the code, enter it on your computer.

Once you finish signing up, verify your email address, and you'll be able to log into your account.

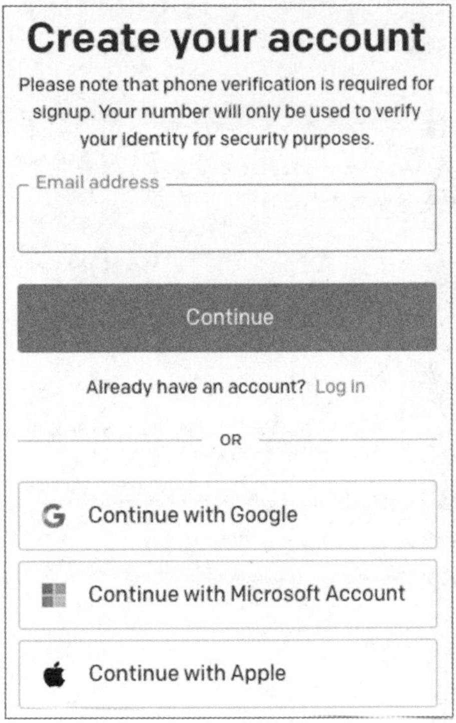

Create your account

Please note that phone verification is required for signup. Your number will only be used to verify your identity for security purposes.

Email address

Continue

Already have an account? Log in

OR

G   Continue with Google

▦   Continue with Microsoft Account

🍎   Continue with Apple

Figure 1-1   On the Create Your Account screen, type your email address and click the Continue button.

Take ChatGPT for a Spin

Once you've set up your research preview account, you're ready to take ChatGPT for a spin.

Log In and Meet the ChatGPT Interface

Log in using your shiny new credentials, and you'll see an interface like that shown in Figure 1-2. The various parts of the interface are straightforward:

- **Sidebar.** This pane appears on the left of the window and gives you access to your chats and your account.

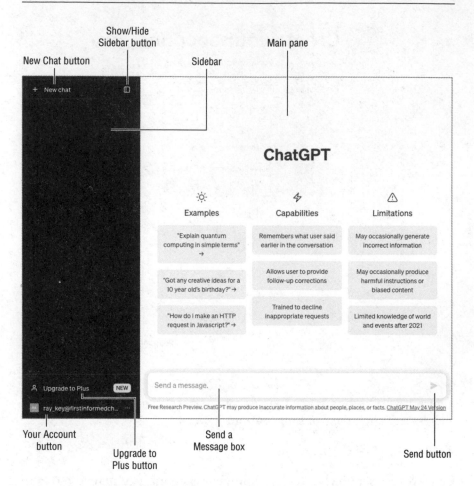

Figure 1-2 The ChatGPT interface is clean and straightforward to navigate.

- **New Chat button.** Click this button to start a new chat. Each chat appears as a button in the sidebar, and you can navigate from chat to chat by clicking the appropriate button.
- **Show/Hide Sidebar button.** Click this button to hide the sidebar when it is displayed; when the sidebar is hidden, click the button to show the sidebar again. If you're working in a small window, hiding the sidebar gives you more space for the active chat. If you're working in a large window, you may just want to leave the sidebar displayed so that you can navigate easily between your chats.

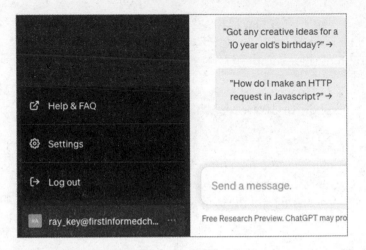

Figure 1-3   **Click the Your Account button to display the control menu.**

- **Main pane.** This area shows your active chat.
- **Send a Message box.** In this box, you type or paste the prompt or information you want to pass to ChatGPT. You then press Enter or click the Send button.
- **Send button.** Click this button to send the contents of the Send a Message box to ChatGPT.
- **Upgrade to Plus button.** Click this button to start the process of upgrading from a free research preview account to a paid Plus account.
- **Your Account button.** This button shows the email address for your account. Click this button to display the control menu shown in Figure 1-3, which gives you access to ChatGPT's Help & FAQ section, lets you access the Settings screen, and enables you to log out.

Give Prompts

Click in the Send a Message box and type what you want to convey to ChatGPT. Here's a quick example to follow. This book shows prompts in boldface, with italics indicating any placeholder text you'll need to supply—for example, in the prompt **What does a *job_title* do?**, you'd replace *job_title* with "lapidary," "hair boiler," "wainwright," or whatever. The book shows ChatGPT's responses in italics, as in the second paragraph of the example.

(PROMPT)   **Explain in 30 words what a mortgage is.**

 A mortgage is a loan provided by a bank or lender to help individuals or businesses purchase property, with the property serving as collateral until the loan is fully repaid.

> **NOTE**   If you need to create a new line, press Shift+Enter. (Don't press Enter on its own because that sends the prompt to ChatGPT.) If you need to paste in something you've copied from elsewhere, give a Paste command. Normally, pressing the standard shortcut, Ctrl+V, is the easiest way. But you can also right-click in the prompt box, and then click Paste on the contextual menu.

Figure 1-4 shows what the ChatGPT window looks like after you give the prompt. As you can see, several new elements appear, enabling you to take further actions:

- **Chat button.** ChatGPT adds a button for the chat to the top of the sidebar and assigns a default name based on your prompt and the response. In the example, ChatGPT names the chat Mortgage Loan Explanation. You can rename the chat by clicking the Rename button.
- **Today section.** ChatGPT breaks up the list of chats in the sidebar by time period—Today, Yesterday, Previous 7 Days, and so on.
- **Rename button.** To rename the chat, click this button, type the new name, and then click the check mark button or press Enter.

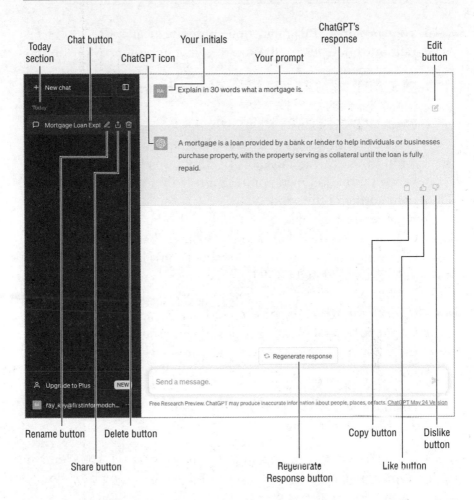

Figure 1-4 When ChatGPT responds to the prompt, you can take several other actions.

- **Share button.** Click this button to start the process of sharing the chat. See the section "Share a Link to a Chat," later in this chapter, for more information.
- **Delete button.** To delete the chat, click this button, and then click the check mark button to its right.
- **Your initials.** This icon shows your initials or the first two letters of your username, making clear the prompt is your input.

- **Your prompt.** The prompt you entered appears.
- **Edit button.** Click this button to edit your prompt. More on this in a moment.
- **ChatGPT icon.** This icon appears to the left of each response from ChatGPT.
- **ChatGPT's response.** ChatGPT's response appears. If the response is long enough to extend past the bottom of the window, scroll down to see more of it. Alternatively, click the Scroll Down button, a down-pointing arrow in a circle in the lower-right corner of the window.
- **Regenerate Response button.** Click this button to make Chat-GPT take another shot at the response. You'd do this if Chat-GPT's response is largely on target but you'd like to see it written differently. After ChatGPT regenerates the response, a Previous (<) button and a Next (>) button appear. Click these buttons to navigate from one response to another.
- **Copy button.** Click this button to copy ChatGPT's response to the Clipboard so that you can paste it elsewhere.
- **Like button.** Click this button to tell ChatGPT that this response gets your approval.
- **Dislike button.** Click this button to let ChatGPT know you don't like this response.

If ChatGPT's response isn't what you're looking for, you can edit the prompt, input more information to refine the prompt, or simply prompt again, as discussed next.

Edit the Prompt, Add Information, or Prompt Again

To edit the prompt, click the Edit button. ChatGPT opens up the prompt for editing (see Figure 1-5), and you can make whatever changes are needed. When you finish, click the Save & Submit button. ChatGPT updates its response.

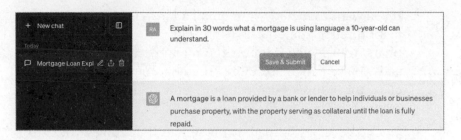

Figure 1-5   **After clicking the Edit button, type the changes to your prompt, and then click the Save & Submit button.**

If you want to leave the prompt as it stands but input more information, type the extra information in the Send a Message box, and then press Enter or click the Send button. Here's an example:

PROMPT   **Please rewrite your response using 60 words and giving an example.**

ChatGPT remembers the content of your active chat, so you can further develop a prompt without having to restate it wholesale. When you switch from one chat to another, ChatGPT loads the content of the active chat, so you can continue the chat.

Alternatively, you can simply enter another prompt, either rephrasing your request (and perhaps giving more detail) or starting another topic.

Share a Link to a Chat

If you want to share a chat with someone, follow these steps:

1. Make the chat active by clicking its button in the sidebar.
2. Click the Share button on the chat's button in the sidebar to open the Share Link to Chat dialog box (see Figure 1-6).
3. Make sure the chat name describes the chat accurately. If not, click the Edit button (the pencil icon) and edit the name or type a better name.

4. If you want to include your email address in the shared information, click the ellipsis (. . .) button, and then click the Share Your Name item on the menu that opens. ChatGPT adds your email address after the chat name. (To remove it, click the ellipsis button again, and then click the Share Anonymously item on the menu.)

5. Click the Copy Link button. ChatGPT copies the link's URL to the Clipboard.

6. Paste the URL into your preferred means of sharing, such as an instant message, an email message, or a Zoom or Slack chat.

The recipient clicks the shared link to open the chat in a browser window. They can then click the Continue This Conversation button to continue the chat.

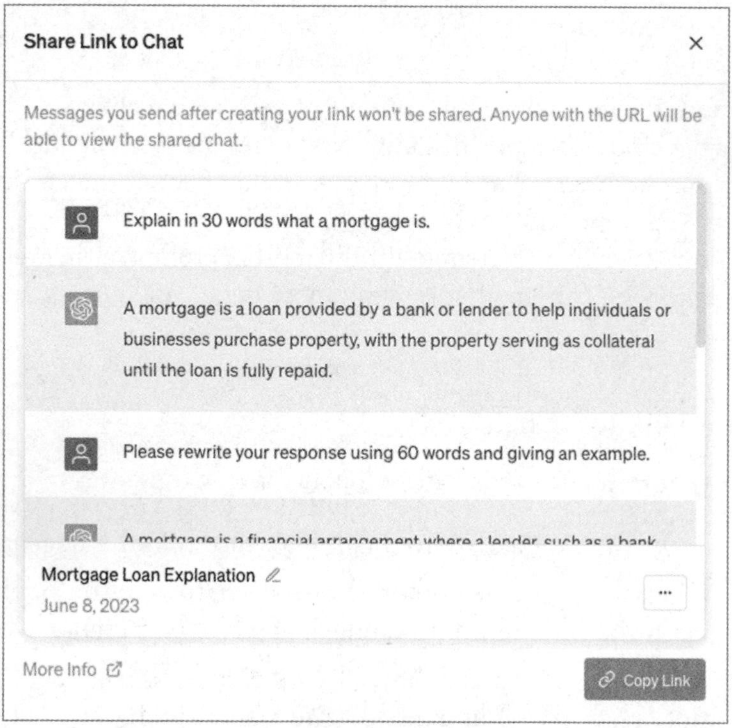

Figure 1-6   Click the Copy Link button in the Share Link to Chat dialog box to share a link to a chat.

Craft Effective Prompts

Creating prompts that make ChatGPT return the results you want is more an art than a science, and you will develop your own techniques for your needs. The example prompts this book provides will steer you in the right direction.

The good news is that ChatGPT's natural-language processing (NLP) is impressive, so you do not have to use set phrasing or put elements in a particular order. Usually, ChatGPT can figure out your meaning; and when it can't, the problem is immediately obvious. For example, if your prompt is unintelligible, ChatGPT asks you to clarify it:

(PROMPT)   **When did industry why nevermore blue focus?**

   I'm sorry, but I'm not sure I understand the question. Could you please provide more context or clarify what you mean by "industry why nevermore blue focus"?

Can You Use Slang? And Should You Give Commands or Make Requests?

Can you use slang when prompting ChatGPT? You betcha! ChatGPT knows a wide range of slang and handles informal input with aplomb. If you prompt ChatGPT "Hit me with five bullets on globalization," you'll get five bullet points; if you prompt "Hit me with a stick," you'll get a response such as "I'm sorry, but I can't fulfill that request." If you use any slang ChatGPT can't figure out, it'll simply tell you.

And whether you give commands (such as "Write a happy cat story") or make requests (such as "Hey, ChatGPT, could you write me a story about a happy cat?"), frankly (my dear), it doesn't make much difference. As long as ChatGPT can understand your prompt, it'll deliver the goods. You don't need to mind your p's and q's; but if you're more comfortable saying "please" and phrasing your prompts as requests, it's fine to do so.

Any time ChatGPT's response to a prompt is not what you're looking for, you can either rephrase the prompt completely or add instructions to make your meaning clearer. Either approach works, so use whichever you prefer.

That said, the clearer and more specific you can make your prompts, the better results you're likely to get. If you can express what you want clearly at the outset, do so.

Staying Within ChatGPT's Query Size Limit

ChatGPT has a query size limit—the maximum amount of text that it can handle at once. The limit is 4096 tokens.

A *token* is a chunk of language that ChatGPT treats as a separate item. This can be anything from a single character to a whole word, depending on the language. So the maximum length of a query is somewhere between 4096 characters and 4096 words. Depending on how long you like your words, 4096 characters is something like 600 words—about two pages of text in an average book. 4096 words is more like 10–12 pages of text in a book. OpenAI mentions 10–15 pages as a guideline amount of text for 4096 tokens, suggesting that a token would typically represent a whole word in English.

Either way, you don't need to worry about the query size limit too much, because ChatGPT warns you if you exceed the limit. When you do exceed the limit, don't use ChatGPT's response, because it will normally be incomplete or off target, as it will be based on only those first 4096 tokens' worth of text. Instead, shorten the query and resubmit it.

Why 4096? Because computers count in binary. 4096 is 2 to the power of 12, or 4×1024.

Evaluate ChatGPT's Output

When ChatGPT returns a response to one of your prompts, read through it carefully. ChatGPT is extremely good at generating text that reads well and appears to be accurate and authoritative, but is in fact neither. So before using ChatGPT's output for any serious purpose, you must evaluate its accuracy.

You're probably familiar with the advice "trust, but verify," the translation of a Russian proverb popularized by President Ronald Reagan while negotiating nuclear disarmament with the Soviet Union. This is good advice in general, but with ChatGPT, you need to take your skepticism to the next level: Distrust, and verify.

If you know the topic about which you're asking ChatGPT, you may be able to verify the content simply by reading through it. But chances are you'll often be asking about something you're not an expert on—that's why you're asking ChatGPT for information rather than reeling it off from memory. For these topics, verify the information by using your favorite search engine or (old-school!) by asking someone who knows the subject area.

> **WARNING**   Don't make the mistake of asking ChatGPT to fact-check its own output. As of this writing, ChatGPT cannot perform serious fact-checking. Asked to confirm a particular piece of information, ChatGPT may assure you it is true, even though it is not.

What Are AI "Hallucinations"?

Like other generative AI transformers, ChatGPT suffers from what are typically referred to as *hallucinations;* you'll also hear the terms "delusions" or "confabulations." These three terms refer to an assertion that an AI makes confidently but that is not true.

Experts disagree about what causes these hallucinations, suggesting inadequate training data, misinterpretation of the training data, a disconnect between the AI's "understanding" of a concept and the user's understanding, or other possibilities. (You'll notice this suggests the user is correct, which ain't necessarily so.)

From your point of view, what causes the hallucinations is likely irrelevant. What matters is that you know that AI hallucinations occur and you need to keep your eyes open for them in the output that ChatGPT returns to you so that they don't trip you up.

Sign Up for a Paid ChatGPT Account

If you're going to use ChatGPT seriously, you should probably sign up for a paid account. The paid plan is called ChatGPT Plus and costs $20 per month as of this writing.

A ChatGPT Plus account has several advantages:

- **You can access the full range of features.** A paid account gives you access to the full range of ChatGPT features, including advanced natural language processing capabilities to help Chat-GPT understand your queries more accurately, more memory to improve performance (particularly on complex queries), and increased computational resources to improve performance and accuracy.
- **You can run more queries and get more detailed responses.** If you have been bumping up against the limits of a free account, moving to a ChatGPT Plus account will enable you to run more queries and get a greater level of detail in the responses.
- **You can customize the ChatGPT interface and functionality.** A ChatGPT Plus account enables you to customize ChatGPT more—but only a bit more. See the section "Customize Your ChatGPT Account," later in this chapter, for more information.
- **You can get priority support.** ChatGPT provides priority support for paid accounts. This means you should be able to get help more quickly when you need it, and the help should be more personalized.
- **You enjoy different licensing and usage rights.** A ChatGPT Plus account brings different licensing and usage rights. In particular, you may be able to use ChatGPT for commercial purposes and you may be able to incorporate ChatGPT into your own products or services.

> **NOTE**   See the Appendix for coverage of what you can and cannot do legally with the output you cause ChatGPT to generate.

Upgrade to a ChatGPT Plus Account

To upgrade to ChatGPT Plus, follow these steps:

1. Log in to your free ChatGPT account as usual.

2. Click the Upgrade to Plus button at the bottom of the sidebar on the left to display the Your Plan dialog box (see Figure 1-7).

Your plan	✕
Free plan	**ChatGPT Plus** USD $20/mo
Your current plan	**Upgrade plan**
⊘ Available when demand is low	⊘ Available even when demand is high
⊘ Standard response speed	⊘ Faster response speed
⊘ Regular model updates	⊘ Priority access to new features
	I need help with a billing issue

Figure 1-7   In the Your Plan dialog box, click the Upgrade Plan button.

3. Click the Upgrade Plan button to display the payment screen.

4. In the Payment Method area, fill in your card information and billing address.

5. If you want to be able to make future payments more quickly by using the Link service, select the Securely Save My Information for 1-Click Checkout check box. If you're like me and can spend money quite fast enough without the Link service, thank you very much, leave this check box clear.

6. If you're paying for ChatGPT for your business, select the I'm Purchasing as a Business check box, and then fill in any extra fields that pop up.

7. Select the You'll Be Charged the Amount Listed Above Every Month Until You Cancel check box. You must select this check box to enable the Subscribe button.

8. Click the Subscribe button.

9. On the Payment Received! screen, click the Continue button.

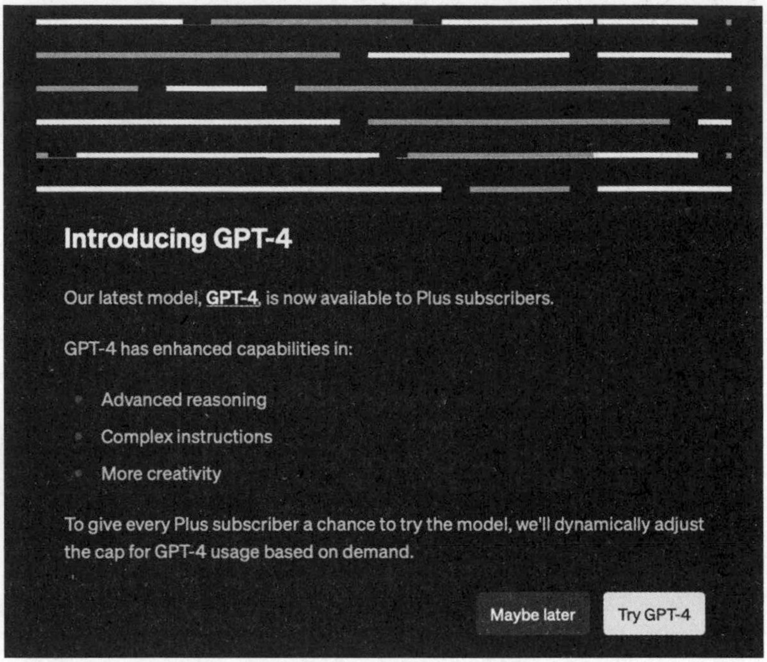

Introducing GPT-4

Our latest model, GPT-4, is now available to Plus subscribers.

GPT-4 has enhanced capabilities in:

- Advanced reasoning
- Complex instructions
- More creativity

To give every Plus subscriber a chance to try the model, we'll dynamically adjust the cap for GPT-4 usage based on demand.

Maybe later   Try GPT-4

Figure 1-8   If OpenAI offers you the chance to try new features, decide whether to go for it.

At this point, you may see a screen offering new features, like the screen in Figure 1-8 offering me the chance to try GPT-4, the latest model. Make your choice and click the appropriate button. As you can no doubt guess, I clicked the Try GPT-4 button rather than the Maybe Later button.

Once you've finished upgrading to a ChatGPT Plus account, you'll notice a couple of changes. Take a look at Figure 1-9.

- Two tabs appear at the top of the screen, enabling you to switch between GPT-3.5 and GPT-4.
- The ChatGPT Plus logo appears as a watermark in the back of the output area.

- Information about restrictions on the latest version may appear above the Send a Message box. For example, in the figure, the readout tells you that GPT-4 has a cap of 25 messages every three hours.

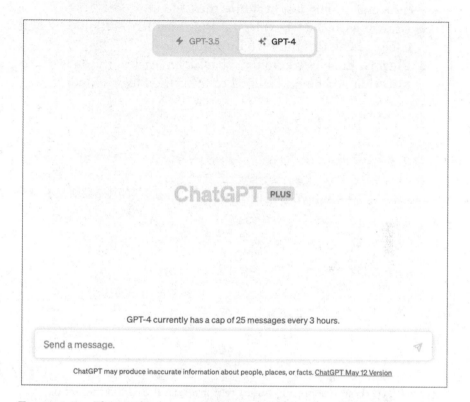

Figure 1-9 **If you chose to enable new features, the tab buttons at the top enable you to switch among them.**

Switch Between ChatGPT Models

With the more advanced tab (such as the GPT-4 tab in the example) selected, click the tab button to display a pop-up menu (see Figure 1-10) containing buttons you can click to switch among ChatGPT's various models. Click the button you want to use, placing a check mark on it (and removing the check mark from whichever other button bore it before). As of this writing, ChatGPT offers these three models:

- **Default.** Runs ChatGPT in its default configuration, without browsing or plug-ins; I call this the Default Model
- **Browse with Bing.** Enables browsing via Microsoft's Bing search engine; I call this the Web Browsing Model
- **Plugins.** Enables you to use ChatGPT plug-ins, third-party features that add functionality; I call this the Plugins Model

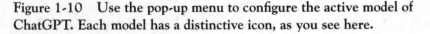

Figure 1-10   Use the pop-up menu to configure the active model of ChatGPT. Each model has a distinctive icon, as you see here.

The icon on the tab button changes to indicate the current mode: one big star and two small stars for the Default Model, a globe icon with one small star for the Web Browsing Model, and a jigsaw piece with one small star for the Plugins Model.

NOTE   Each chat uses a single model, such as the Default Model or the Web Browsing Model. You set the model at the beginning of the chat; once the chat is underway, you can't switch it to a different model. To use a different model, start a new chat.

Once you've switched to the Web Browsing Model, a readout appears to the right of the ChatGPT icon as it processes its response, showing you that ChatGPT is browsing the web. When ChatGPT finishes browsing, a drop-down list replaces the readout. You can open this drop-down list to view the actions ChatGPT took on the web (see Figure 1-11).

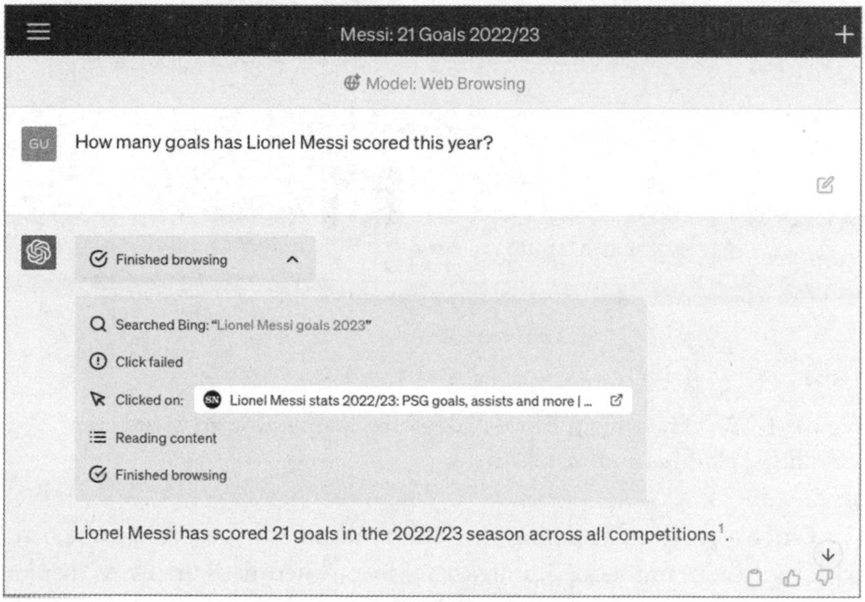

Figure 1-11   In the Web Browsing Model, open the drop-down list to see the actions ChatGPT took on the web in response to your prompt.

When you switch to the Plugins Model, ChatGPT displays a drop-down list below the tab buttons showing which plug-ins you've enabled. At first, the drop-down list will show No Plugins Enabled. Click the drop-down list's arrow to display the available plug-ins, and then click the one you want. If there are no plug-ins yet, click the Plugin Store button to display the About Plugins dialog box, and then click the OK button to display the Plugin Store dialog box (see Figure 1-12). Here, you can browse or search for plug-ins. Click the Install button to install each plug-in you want to add.

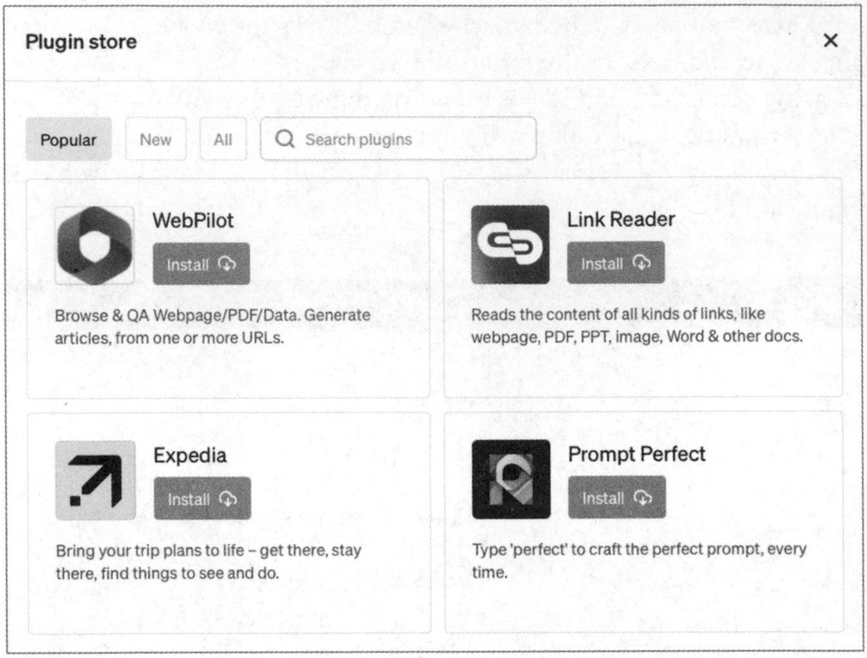

Figure 1-12   The Plugin Store dialog box enables you to browse or search for plug-ins and install them.

Once you've added plug-ins, the readout shows icons indicating which of them are loaded. Click the drop-down list's arrow to display the list of plug-ins (see Figure 1-13). You can then select or clear their check boxes to load or unload the plug-ins.

Customize Your ChatGPT Account

Whether you have a free ChatGPT account or a paid account, you can customize it a little. A ChatGPT Plus account offers a few more options than a free account.

To customize your account, click the button bearing your account name at the bottom of the left pane. In the menu that pops up, click Settings to display the Settings dialog box. The General pane appears at first (see Figure 1-14); you can navigate to the other panes by clicking their tabs on the left. As of this writing, the General pane and the Data Controls pane appear for both free accounts and paid accounts, but the Beta Features pane appears only for paid accounts.

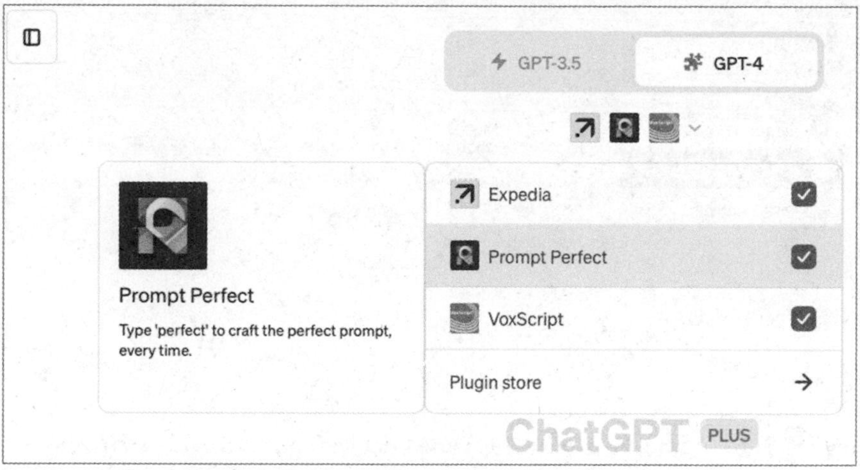

Figure 1-13 With the Plugins Model active, you can load and unload plug-ins from the drop-down list.

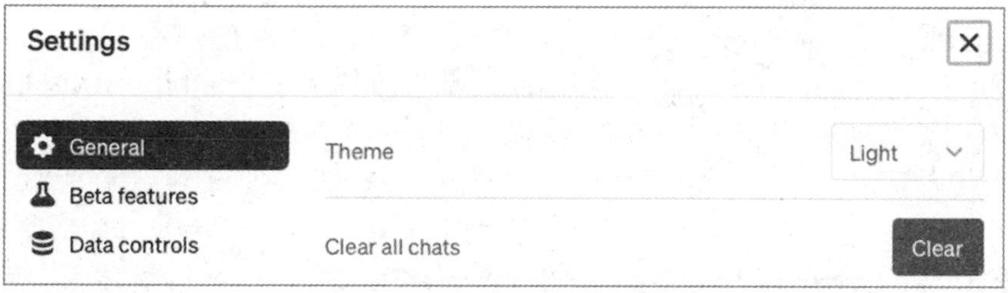

Figure 1-14 The General pane of the Settings dialog box enables you to choose the theme and clear all your chats.

Choose Settings in the General Pane

The General pane enables you to take two actions:

- **Select the theme.** Click the Theme drop-down list, and then click Light, Dark, or System. Light is the theme shown in this book; Dark may feel easier on your eyes when you are computing in low light; and System uses your computer's system setting of Light or Dark theme.
- **Clear your chat history.** Click the Clear button. ChatGPT gets rid of the chats without confirmation.

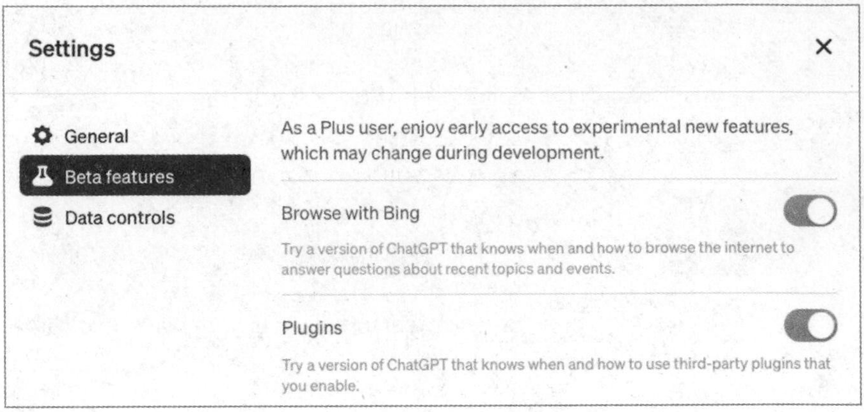

Figure 1-15   The Beta Features pane enables you to turn the current beta features on or off.

Choose Settings in the Beta Features Pane

The Beta Features pane enables ChatGPT Plus users to enable and disable beta (pre-release) features. Figure 1-15 shows the Beta Features pane as of this writing, which lets you (well, me) enable or disable the Browse with Bing feature and the Plugins feature by setting their switches.

Choose Settings in the Data Controls Pane

The Data Controls pane (see Figure 1-16) contains the most important settings:

- **Chat History & Training.** Set this switch to On (green) if you want to save new chats to your chat history. This is usually helpful, especially as you can delete individual chats when you no longer need them.

> **NOTE**   If you save new chats to your chat history, ChatGPT uses them to help improve its language model. If you don't save new chats to your chat history, ChatGPT keeps them for up to 30 days before deleting them.

- **Shared Links.** Click the Manage button to display the Share Links dialog box, which enables you to see your shared links, call up their chats, and delete the links.
- **Export Data.** Click this button if you want to export all your ChatGPT data to a file that you can download via a link that OpenAI sends to your email.
- **Delete Account.** Click this button to start the process of deleting your ChatGPT account.
- **Enable Two-Factor Authentication.** Click this button to start setting up two-factor authentication to protect your ChatGPT account from intrusion.

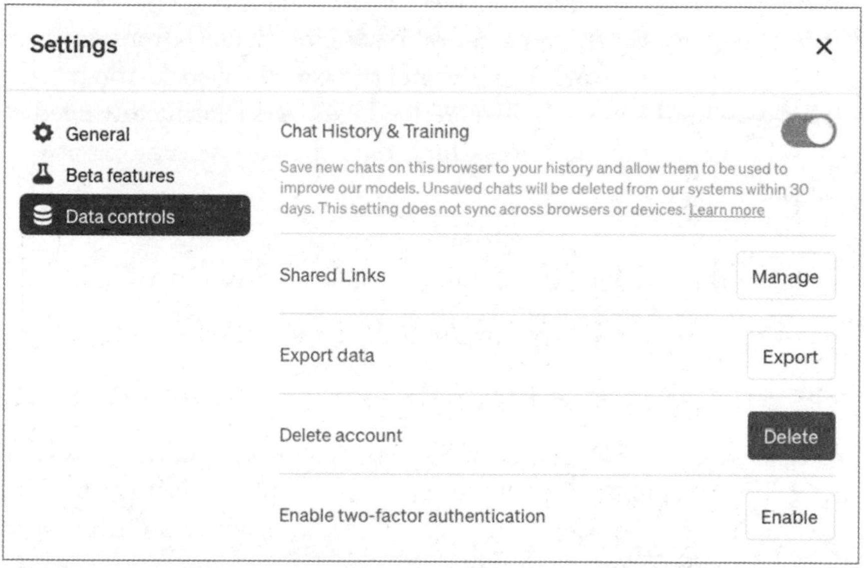

Figure 1-16   The Data Controls pane lets you configure your chat history and training, shared links, data export, and two-factor authentication. You can also delete your ChatGPT account.

Set Up ChatGPT on Your Devices

Once you've created your ChatGPT account, you can access Chat-GPT by opening a browser on any device and entering your credentials. If you use multiple computers—for example, a laptop and a desktop—you'll likely want to save your credentials on each of them so you can fire up ChatGPT without having to retype them for each session.

You can use a browser on your phone or tablet as well, but OpenAI provides a ChatGPT app for iOS, iPadOS, and Android. The app is easier to use on a small screen, so you'll likely want to use it.

WARNING   If you decide to install a ChatGPT app, make sure you get the official app from OpenAI. Various third-party apps are available, many of which charge extra fees. Before installing any of these apps, you should look into the app developers' privacy policy—for example, scrutinize the App Privacy section of the app's page on the App Store, paying particular attention to the Data Used to Track You box and the Data Linked to You box. It may be hard to tell which data the developers legitimately need for the app to function and which data they are harvesting as a bonus.

Install the ChatGPT App on Your iPhone or iPad

To install the ChatGPT app on your iPhone or iPad, follow these steps:

1. Display the Home screen. On an iPhone or iPad that has Face ID, swipe up to display the app switcher, then tap at the bottom of the screen. On an iPhone or iPad that has Touch ID, press the Home button.
2. Tap the App Store icon to open the App Store app.
3. Tap the Search button on the right end of the tab bar at the bottom of the screen to display the Search screen.
4. Tap in the Search field and type **openai chatgpt**. A list of results appears.
5. Tap the "openai chatgpt official" result. A screen of supposedly matching apps appears (see the left screen in Figure 1-17).
6. Tap the ChatGPT app from OpenAI to display its screen (shown on the right in Figure 1-17).

7. Verify that the Developer readout shows OpenAI.

8. Tap the Get button, and then confirm the installation in the App Store dialog that opens. For example, you may need to double-click the iPhone's Side button.

9. Once the installation finishes, tap the Open button on the ChatGPT screen in the App Store app to launch the app. If you've already left the App Store app, tap the ChatGPT icon on the iPhone's Home screen.

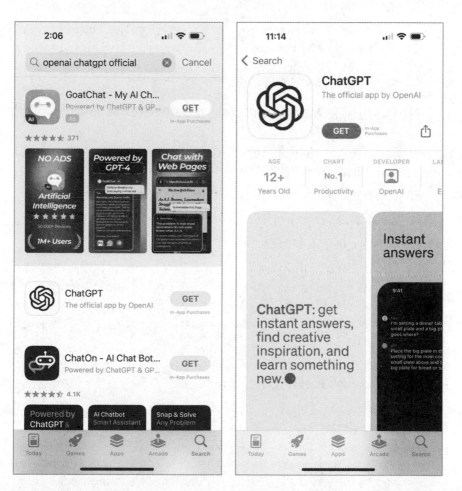

Figure 1-17   Make sure you choose the ChatGPT app from OpenAI rather than a third-party app. On the app's screen (right), tap the Get button to start the installation.

Skip ahead to the section "Sign In to Your ChatGPT Account," later in this chapter.

Install the ChatGPT App on Your Android Device

To install ChatGPT on your Android phone or tablet, follow these steps:

1. Display the Home screen by swiping up from the bottom of the screen and then tapping Home.

2. If the Play Store icon appears directly on the Home screen, tap it there. Otherwise, drag your finger up the Home screen to display the App Drawer, and then tap the Play Store icon. The Play Store app opens.

3. Tap in the Search field and type **openai chatgpt**. A list of results appears.

4. Tap the "openai chatgpt official" result to display a list of matching apps.

5. Tap the ChatGPT app from OpenAI to display its screen.

6. Double-check that the Developer readout shows OpenAI.

7. Tap the Install button.

8. Once the installation finishes, tap the Open button on the ChatGPT screen in the App Store app to launch the app. If you've already left the App Store app, return to the Home screen, open the App Drawer, and then tap the ChatGPT icon.

Sign In to Your ChatGPT Account

The first time you run the ChatGPT app, it walks you through signing in to your ChatGPT account. Follow these steps:

1. On the splash screen shown on the left in Figure 1-18, tap the Log In button. Your device displays the Welcome Back screen in the default browser, as shown on the right in Figure 1-18.

2. Tap the Email Address box and type your email address.

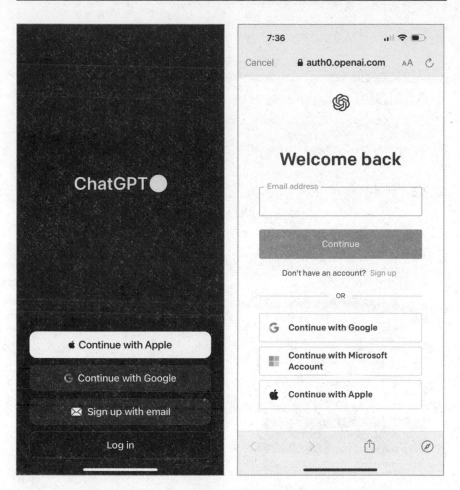

Figure 1-18   Tap the Log In button on the splash screen (left) to log in with your existing ChatGPT account. On the Welcome Back screen, type your email address and tap the Continue button.

3. Tap the Continue button. The Enter Your Password screen appears.

4. Type your password.

5. Tap the Continue button. The Welcome to ChatGPT screen appears, as shown on the left in Figure 1-19.

6. Read the information and warnings, and then tap the Continue button.

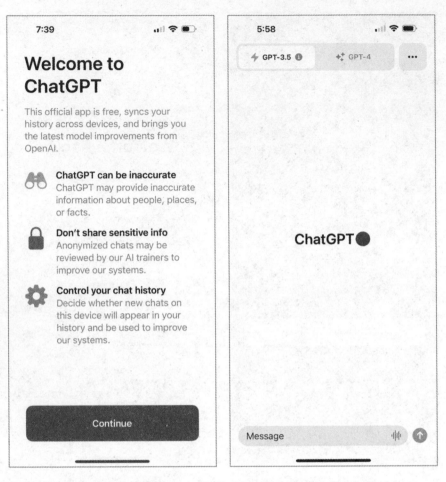

Figure 1-19   On the Welcome to ChatGPT screen (left), read the information and tap the Continue button. When the ChatGPT screen (right) appears, you're in business.

The ChatGPT screen appears, and you can start using ChatGPT. But first you might want to take a minute or two to configure Chat-GPT, as explained next.

Configure ChatGPT on Your Device

To configure ChatGPT on your device, tap the Menu button (the ellipsis), and then tap Settings on the menu that pops up. The Settings screen appears, as shown on the left in Figure 1-20.

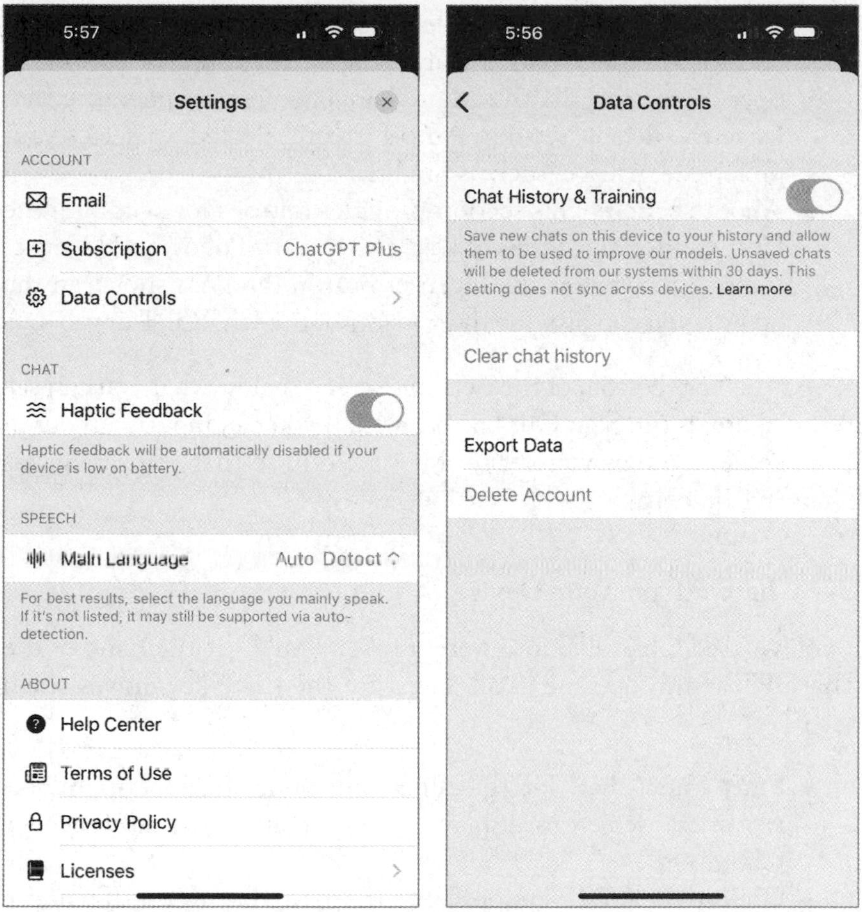

Figure 1-20   You can configure several settings for ChatGPT on the Settings screen (left). Tap the Data Controls button to display the Data Controls screen (right).

The Settings screen contains four sections: Account, Chat, Speech, and About. Here's what you can do in them:

- **Account section.** The Email button shows the email address associated with your ChatGPT account. The Subscription button shows your subscription type, such as ChatGPT Plus. The Data Controls button displays the Data Controls screen (shown on the right in Figure 1-20). Here you can enable or disable chat history and training, clear your chat history, export your data, or delete your account.

- **Chat section.** Set the Haptic Feedback switch to On or Off to control whether ChatGPT gives haptic (vibrating) feedback.
- **Speech section.** In the Main Language pop-up menu, either leave the default setting, Auto-Detect, selected, or select your preferred language, such as English.
- **About section.** This section provides buttons for accessing the Help Center, the Terms of Use, the Privacy Policy, and Licenses information. Below the Licenses button (and not shown in the figure), you can also see the version of the ChatGPT app.

At the very bottom of the Settings screen, below what you can see in the figure, is the Sign Out button, which you can tap to sign out of your account. You may prefer to stay signed in so that you can access ChatGPT quickly.

Use ChatGPT on Your Device

If you've used ChatGPT in a web browser, you'll get the hang of the ChatGPT app in no time at all. Here are the three key moves you'll need:

- **Start a new chat.** Tap the ellipsis button in the upper-right corner of the screen to display the menu, and then tap the New Chat item.
- **Choose the GPT version.** Tap the appropriate tab button at the top of the screen.
- **Navigate between chats.** Tap the ellipsis button to display the menu, and then tap the History item to show the History pane. The pane occupies the lower half of the screen by default, but you can expand it by dragging its title bar up the screen. Browse or search to locate the chat you want to make active, and then tap its button.

2

ChatGPT Prompts for Getting a Job

IF YOU'RE LOOKING for a job, waste no time in leveraging the help that ChatGPT can offer. In this chapter, you'll find prompts you can use to get help creating your resume and polishing it, seek career guidance, and dig into your target industries and potential employers. You'll also find prompts for enlisting ChatGPT's assistance in writing cover letters, preparing yourself for interviews, and following up with your interviewers via mail or email.

Get Help Writing and Polishing Your Resume

Do you hate writing resumes? Join the club! Setting down your life-to-date and goals on a sheet of paper—okay, in a word processing document—is a weird combination of mechanical drudgery and marketing spin that comes naturally to very few people.

ChatGPT can help. A lot.

What you'd probably like is for you to give ChatGPT a quick prompt such as "Write a one-page resume for me" and have it crank out your ticket to a dream job. But as you can imagine, it's not that simple, because you must give ChatGPT the raw information to work with.

Once you've done that, ChatGPT *can* write the resume for you. You can then hone the resume, either on your own or with ChatGPT's help, and format it so it's ready for use.

Let's take it from the top.

Gather the Information for the Resume

Start by gathering the information for the resume and entering it into a word processing document. The following list breaks down what you need for a fairly standard resume. If your resume needs other categories of information, include those, too.

- **Contact Information:**
  o Your full name
  o Your mailing address
  o Your professional phone number
  o Your professional email address

- **Objective Statement:**
  o Spell out your career goals.
  o Explain how you would be a good fit for the job.

- **Experience:**
  o List your job history (most recent first).
  o Include the company or organization, your job title, and your start and end dates.
  o List your key responsibilities.
  o List your main achievements.

- **Education:**
  o List your colleges and schools (most recent first).
  o Include your degrees, GPA, and noteworthy coursework.

- **Skills:**
  o List your skills relevant to the job.
  o Include hard skills, such as foreign language proficiency and knowledge of leading software.
  o Mention soft skills such as negotiation or problem solving.

- **Certifications and Licenses:**
  - o Include relevant certifications, such as Microsoft Office certifications.
  - o Include professional licenses, such as CPA.

- **Volunteer Work:**
  - o If you have performed volunteer work that showcases skills relevant to the job, include it in this section.
  - o Include details of the organization, the dates, and any key takeaways, such as leadership experience.

- **References:**
  - o If the job listing asks for references, provide the names and contact information for the specified number of referees.
  - o Otherwise, state "References available on request" and do not list referees.

Get ChatGPT to Write the Resume

Once you've gathered the information in the previous section, select it in the word processing document and copy it to the Clipboard (for example, press Ctrl+C). Go to your ChatGPT window and type a prompt such as this:

(PROMPT) **Write a resume using the following information:**

You could also give a more specific prompt, telling ChatGPT specific areas to focus on. For example, you might ask for bullet points showcasing your achievements:

(PROMPT) **Write a resume using the following information. Include three bullet points for three key achievements.**

For either of these examples, press Shift+Enter to insert a line break after the prompt, press Ctrl+V to paste in the information, and then press Enter to execute the prompt.

ChatGPT returns a formatted resume based on the information, prefacing it with a paragraph explaining that this is a formatted resume and following it with a paragraph advising you to tailor the resume to each job you're applying for.

At this point, you can take the following actions:

- Click the Regenerate Response button to have ChatGPT rewrite the resume entirely.
- Prompt ChatGPT to rewrite part of the resume (see the next section).
- Customize the resume to suit a particular job description (see the section "Customize the Resume to Suit a Job Description," later in this chapter).
- Click the Copy button, paste the resume into a word processing app, and tweak it as necessary. Start by removing the opening and closing paragraphs.

Ask ChatGPT to Rewrite the Resume

ChatGPT may hit the resume clean out of the park on the first shot, but more likely, it'll get you on one of the bases, and parts of the resume will need rewriting. If only minor tweaks are needed, you can do them yourself. But for more extensive changes or for any restructuring, have ChatGPT do the lion's share of the work.

> **NOTE** This section assumes that you are still working in the chat in which you created the resume. If so, ChatGPT still has the resume information available, so you don't need to paste it in. If you're in a different chat, either go back to the previous chat, or paste in the resume after the prompt.

You could use a prompt like this to add information:

 Rewrite that resume, adding my Doctorate in Computer Science from Stanford in 2020.

In this example, ChatGPT added not only a section for the doctorate to the Education section of the resume, but also a brief mention to the Objective section.

Similarly, you might add a References section and take out the Objective section:

 Add to that resume a References section saying that references are available on request. Take out the Objective section.

ChatGPT does that, too, with its unfailing good humor.

You might also ask for a change of focus in the resume. For example:

 Rewrite the resume to showcase my programming skills, my problem-solving ability, and my troubleshooting acumen.

You can also have ChatGPT make more mechanical alterations, such as changing the length of the resume. You might need to do this when a job advertisement specifies a maximum or minimum length. For example:

 Make the resume five lines shorter.

Or:

 Make the resume 75 words longer.

Get ChatGPT to Suggest Improvements to the Resume

After creating a resume, either with ChatGPT's help or on your own, you can ask ChatGPT to read it and suggest improvements. Here is an example:

 Read that resume, identify any omissions, and tell me how to improve it.

> **NOTE**   If you've been working on the resume with ChatGPT in the active chat, ChatGPT uses the most recent version of the resume. If not, either go back to the resume chat or paste in the resume after the prompt.

ChatGPT immediately returns an assessment of the resume, noting any obvious omissions and suggesting possible improvements. ChatGPT noted that my sample resume was missing an Objective statement (because we took it out in the previous section); suggested omitting the References section, because employers will assume candidates can provide them; and recommended adding information on awards, languages, volunteer work, publications, and conferences.

You can use prompts such as those in the previous section to make these changes.

Customize the Resume to Suit a Job Description

By this point, you should have gotten your resume into good shape for general use. But you shouldn't be sending out the same resume for each job application. Instead, you should customize your resume to suit the job description as well as possible.

ChatGPT can customize your resume quickly and neatly. You'll usually want to work in three windows (or tabs, depending on the apps you're using):

- Have ChatGPT open in one window.
- Open your resume in Microsoft Word, Google Docs, or whatever in a second window.
- Call up the job description in a third window.

Once you've got everything open and in view, give a prompt along these lines:

(PROMPT)   **Customize my resume to suit this job description for the** *job_title* **position.**

NOTE For each of these prompts, type the prompt, entering the job title where the placeholder appears. Press Shift+Enter to insert a line break, and then paste in your resume. Press Shift+Enter again to insert another line break, and then paste in the job description. Then press Enter to run the prompt.

ChatGPT swiftly returns a customized version of your resume, bookending it with brief explanations such as these:

Certainly, based on the job description you provided, I've tailored your resume to better fit the requirements and responsibilities of a Senior Python Programmer role:

. . .

This version of your resume focuses more on your Python program-ming skills, leadership experience, and ability to collaborate with various stakeholders, which align with the requirements of the job description provided.

Create a Resume Summary

ChatGPT is great at creating resume summaries to a specified length from your resume. Here are two examples of prompts you might use:

 Create a 100-word summary that highlights my skills and experiences pertaining to a *job_title* role.

Write a 200-word summary focusing on my proven ability to create sales leads and increase revenue.

(continued)

You don't need to specify the length. You might prefer to let ChatGPT determine the length from the material it finds— for example:

 Generate a summary that showcases my programming experience migrating COBOL systems to modern platforms.

If necessary, you can then tell ChatGPT to rewrite the summary to a specific length:

 Rewrite that summary so it is 150 words long.

Make ChatGPT Your Career Guidance Counselor

If you have a career guidance counselor, you'll want to make the most of their advice and (let's hope) wisdom to set you on a suitable career path. But if you don't have a career guidance counselor, ChatGPT can step into that role.

ChatGPT can help you identify careers that match your skills and interests, tell you what a particular career involves, and also suggest what skills and certifications you might need for a career in a particular field.

Identify Careers That Match Your Skills and Interests

If you are looking for a career, tell ChatGPT what skills and interests you have. For example:

 Suggest five careers for me to consider. I am an English speaker who is fluent in Spanish and German. I enjoy helping people, seeing new places, and solving problems.

ChatGPT responded to this prompt with careers ranging from Foreign Service Officer/Diplomat to International Aid/Development

Worker, with Translator/Interpreter and Multilingual Tour Guide along the way.

Or you might prompt ChatGPT to identify jobs in particular areas. For example:

(PROMPT) **What careers should I look at that combine audio engineering with entertainment in New York?**

ChatGPT suggested various types of Sound Engineer—Live, Recording, and Post-Production—along with Audio Designer for Video Games and Foley Artist. (Foley, named after the U.S. film technician Jack rather than detective Axel, is work adding recorded sound effects to film footage.)

Explore Careers That Interest You

If you already know what careers interest you, use ChatGPT to research them further. Here are examples of prompts you might use:

(PROMPT) **Describe the typical career path of a Realtor.**

ChatGPT tells you about the minimum educational qualification, about getting a real estate license, joining a real estate brokerage, and so on.

(PROMPT) **Please tell me about entry-level positions in investment banking.**

ChatGPT returned a list of positions including Investment Banking Analyst, Sales and Trading Analyst, and Risk Analyst. It also mentioned Investment Banking Associate, noting that the position is entry-level provided you have an MBA.

(PROMPT) **What is the typical starting salary for a metal machining setter?**

ChatGPT returned the median annual wage for metal and plastic machine workers, which was $37,370 in May 2020.

Learn What Skills and Certifications You Need for a Particular Field

If you're looking to go into a particular field, you can get advice from ChatGPT on the skills and certifications you might want to acquire. For example, say you're interested in a clinical data manager role:

(PROMPT) **What certifications should a clinical data manager hold?**

ChatGPT returned information about certifications ranging from Certified Clinical Data Manager (CCDM) through Project Management Professional (PMP).

(PROMPT) **What personal skills does a Realtor need for success?**

ChatGPT returned a range of skills including communication, negotiation, networking, organization, and problem solving.

(PROMPT) **What education will I need for a career in hotel management?**

ChatGPT gave me the lowdown on degrees in Hospitality Management, details on certifications such as Certified Hotel Administrator, and mentioned the value of internships and work experience.

Jobs Involving ChatGPT and Other AI

As you know, AI is a rapidly growing area. That means more and more people are working in AI—at least until AI starts running itself—and performing increasingly specialized roles.

This sidebar gives you a quick look at some of the jobs that involve working on or with AI. It's not exhaustive—especially as more roles have likely been invented since this book rolled off the presses.

If you're just getting started with AI and do not have formal training in a related discipline, look at jobs such as these:

- **Prompt Engineer.** Also called an "AI whisperer," a prompt engineer is someone who creates effective prompts for getting the desired results from a language model. This is essentially what you're learning from this book—so after you develop your skills, you might be able to slide straight into this role.
- **AI Ethicist.** If you have a background in philosophy or ethics, this might be the job for you—thinking deeply about the role that AI should play in companies or government and developing guidelines for AI applications.
- **Data Analyst.** If you're adept with tools such as Microsoft Excel, Power Query, and Power BI, this might be a great role for you. Adding AI can turbocharge both your research and your results.
- **Business Intelligence Developer.** This role uses AI to harvest complex data sets, analyze them, and develop strategic insights to guide business decisions. Business intelligence developer can be a natural career progression up from data analyst.
- **AI Consultant.** An AI consultant advises companies and organizations on the benefits AI may offer them and how best to implement AI. You need a good high-level understanding of AI but not in-depth technical knowledge.

(continued)

- **AI Product Manager.** An AI product manager works with AI engineers and data scientists to define a viable AI product, launch the project, and bring it to fruition. For this role, too, you need a good high-level understanding of AI but only some technical knowledge—the nitty without the gritty, as it were.

If you have more experience in AI or formal training in a related discipline, look at jobs such as these:

- **AI Specialist.** This job title can mean pretty much whatever a company wants it to mean—so if you're not sure what an employer is looking for, ask for specifics. But usually an AI specialist is someone who applies AI to a specific field, such as finance (for example, high-frequency trading) or logistics.
- **AI Software Developer.** This is pretty much what it says: An AI software developer designs, develops, and sometimes maintains AI software.
- **Machine Learning Engineer.** A machine learning engineer builds and maintains computer systems for machine-learning projects. You'd typically need a background in programming, computer science, and hardware.
- **AI Research Scientist.** An AI research scientist works to advance the development and deployment of AI in general rather than in a specific setting. Serious research usually requires serious hardware, which involves serious costs—so typically an AI research scientist would work in an academic setting (did I hear you mutter "MIT"?) or in the research and development department of a large company.
- **Natural Language Processing Engineer.** Wrestling with natural language processing (NLP), such an engineer works on enabling AI to understand human language and communicate with humans in return.

Research Your Target Industries and Potential Employers

By this stage, you should have a rough idea of the type of position you want and the industry or area in which you'd like to work. Your next move should be to research your target industries and identify potential employers.

> **TIP**
>
> **Make Sure ChatGPT's Web Browsing Model Is Enabled**
>
> As of this writing, ChatGPT operates by default using a huge but still limited database rather than searching the web for the latest information. Given this, be aware that the information ChatGPT provides may be out of date. ChatGPT typically gives you a cutoff date—for example, "Here are a few examples as of my last update in September 2021."
>
> To get the latest information, enable ChatGPT's web-browsing capability. As of this writing, this feature is in beta. To enable it, click the New Chat button in the left column to start a new chat, and then click the GPT-4 button to switch to GPT-4 mode. Hover the pointer over the GPT-4 button to pop up a menu, and then click the Browse with Bing button to place a check mark to the right of the text. (If the check mark is already there, you're all set.)

Here are three examples of prompts you might use:

PROMPT **Which hedge funds practice ethical investment?**

ChatGPT consulted Bing for a few minutes, and then produced a short list of hedge funds and investment funds.

PROMPT **Explain the McDonald's business model to me.**

ChatGPT fills you in about the company's two primary segments, franchised restaurants (the majority) and company-operated restaurants.

 Tell me about the different divisions of Boeing.

ChatGPT delivered a breakdown on Boeing Commercial Airplanes; Boeing Defense, Space & Security; and Boeing Global Services.

Get Help Writing Cover Letters or Email Messages

For most job applications, you'll want to include a cover letter or email message along with your customized resume. Don't dash off a cursory missive just to get the application on its way. Instead, treat the letter or message as another opportunity to showcase your professionalism and communication skills—and do enlist ChatGPT's help.

Here is an example of using a prompt for a cover letter to a fictitious publishing company:

PROMPT **Write a cover letter for a job application for the position Editorial Assistant at the company Parados Press. Include my contact information from my resume.**

Here is the company information: Parados Press, 4152 Acacia, City of Industry, CA 90601. Address the letter to Jaclyn Ramirez, HR Director.

In this example, I asked ChatGPT to pick up my contact information from my resume, which we had worked on together earlier in the active chat. If you're in a different chat, either switch back to the chat containing the resume or enter the information yourself.

ChatGPT generated a straightforward and largely suitable letter, including skills appropriate to the position—some skills derived from the resume, but others ChatGPT had cooked up itself. ChatGPT also decided that Parados Press published "original, thought-provoking literature," which would be nice were it true.

So I asked for a rewrite, using this prompt:

 PROMPT **Rewrite the cover letter to include information about the type of works Parados Press publishes. The works cover military technology for offense and defense, specializing in medieval siege machines and defenses against them.**

ChatGPT delivered a terrific rewrite, smoothly changing the focus to military history and technology.

I then asked ChatGPT to change the cover letter to an email message:

PROMPT **Change the cover letter to an email message with a maximum length of 175 words.**

Again, ChatGPT delivered a good, clear result.

TIP Even when ChatGPT gives you what you need, see if there's room for improvement. For example, you might use prompts such as these:

PROMPT **Tell me three ways to improve that email message.**

Or:

PROMPT **Read that cover letter and tell me how to enhance it.**

In this case, ChatGPT suggested adding specific achievements (including metrics), demonstrating knowledge of the target company (such as referencing one of Parados Press' books), and expressing greater enthusiasm for the possibility of working there.

Prepare for an Interview

For most people, the interview is the hardest part of the process of getting a job. The interviewer or interviewers can ask you any of a near-infinite range of questions, and you're supposed to produce sensible answers that present you and your skills in a good light. On the spot. With a polite smile.

ChatGPT can't sit at the interview for you, but it can help you practice your answers, albeit in writing rather than in speech. You can set up the interview using an "act as" prompt such as this, spelling out exactly what you want ChatGPT to do:

Act as an interviewer for the position Editorial Assistant at Parados Press. I am the candidate for the position. Reply only as the interviewer, asking me a single question at a time and waiting for me to answer. After I answer, ask me the next question. I start by saying "Hello! How are you today?"

Hello! I'm doing well, thank you. I hope you are too.

Let's get started with our interview. Can you begin by telling me a bit more about your experience with editing and how it has prepared you for the role of Editorial Assistant?

I replied, giving suitable information, and the interview proceeded from there.

This is just the start. You can get more sophisticated—for example, in the same chat:

I'd like to practice interviewing again. This time, please act as three interviewers: Jaclyn Ramirez, HR Director and the lead interviewer; Mike Li, the Editorial Director; and Billie Schmidt, an Editorial Assistant. Have one interviewer ask me a question; let me answer; and then switch among interviewers as might happen during an interview. Specify which interviewer is speaking. I start by saying "Good morning!"

As the lead interviewer, Jaclyn Ramirez returned my greeting and kicked off the interview; I answered; Mike Li asked the next question; and the interview continued from there.

You can also get ChatGPT to ask you about specific topics:

Let's resume our one-on-one interview where we left it. I'd like you to ask me questions about how I have dealt with awkward colleagues. Please start now.

Absolutely, let's continue. Could you share a specific instance where you had to deal with a difficult or awkward colleague and how you managed the situation?

NOTE Practicing interviews with ChatGPT can be a great way to think through your responses to possible questions, but you should include spoken practice as much as possible. Create a list of questions (with ChatGPT's help) and ask a family member or friend to run you through them.

Write a Post-Interview Email Message or Letter

After your interview, follow up with the interviewer or interviewers and thank them for their time. You can also remind them of a memorable point that will help them distinguish you from your competitors, give details on an issue you left unresolved, or ask follow-up questions.

Email is usually best because it will reach them sooner, but for some applications you may prefer to send a letter.

Here's an example of a prompt for an email message:

Write a follow-up email message 150 words max to Jaclyn Ramirez thanking her for the interview for the Editorial Assistant position at Parados Press yesterday. I was delighted to meet her and Mike Li and enjoyed our discussion about the comparative merits of trebuchets and ballistas.

The resulting message covered the right ground but was too formal—stodgy, perhaps. So I asked:

 Rewrite that message to make it less formal and more engaging.

But that version came out too casual—chummy enough to make HR cringe. So I tried a third time:

 Please rewrite the message to make it a little more formal than that but less formal than the first version.

And this time it was just right, and Goldilocks was happy.

3

ChatGPT Prompts for Managing Your Work and Schedule

IF YOU MANAGE your own work and schedule, make sure you leverage ChatGPT's powerful capabilities for lightening your load. By using the right prompts, you can get ChatGPT to streamline your meetings and deal with the business they generate, such as agendas beforehand and reminders and follow-ups afterward. ChatGPT can also help you get your email under control and assist you with planning and arranging travel.

People who use ChatGPT for these tasks describe the resulting boost as being as though they've hired an intern or an assistant. On the plus side, ChatGPT costs far less than an intern (assuming that you pay your interns — and that you pay for ChatGPT), has near-infinite patience, and won't show up to work late or blitzed. On the downside, ChatGPT won't fetch your coffee — but you can prompt it for tips on how to brew better coffee, how to cut down your caffeine intake, or even both.

Streamline Your Meetings

Meetings, meetings, meetings — seems we simply can't live without them, though many of us sure would like to. Just think how much your productivity would soar if you could flat-out abolish meetings . . .

Okay, stop thinking about that now and get back to work. Abolishing meetings is not on the agenda. What *is* on the agenda is having ChatGPT streamline your meetings so that you can glide through them with minimal resistance and effort.

In this section, we'll look at five ways in which ChatGPT can help you with your meetings:

- Scheduling your meetings
- Setting agendas for your meetings
- Preparing for your meetings and performing research
- Organizing and structuring your meeting notes
- Following up after meetings

Schedule Your Meetings

When you need to schedule a meeting, prompt ChatGPT with the relevant information. For most meetings, that means the following details:

- The meeting participants
- The dates and times the participants are available
- The meeting's purpose (such as Product Development or Company Rightsizing)
- The meeting's duration
- The location or platform you'll use (such as Conference Room B or Microsoft Teams)
- Your specific requirements for the meeting

Here's an example of a prompt you might use:

 Schedule me a meeting with Jill Perez, Steve Clark, and Cookie Murphy. Pick a date and time using the availability information included below. We need to talk about next year's budget. We'll meet for about an hour using Zoom. I'd like you to write an invitation I can send out.

You'd then press Shift+Enter to insert a line break, and then press Ctrl+V to paste in the schedule information for the participants.

Based on the availability you provided, the best time slot where everyone is available would be Tuesday from 2 p.m. to 3 p.m. Here's a draft invitation you could send out:

Subject: Budget Meeting for Next Year

Dear Jill, Steve, and Cookie, . . .

The invitation was fine, except that I had forgotten something. So:

That looks good, but please ask Jill to send all of us the budget guidelines via email as soon as possible.

Of course. Here's the revised invitation: . . .

Set Meeting Agendas

For any but the simplest or most informal meeting, it usually pays to create a formal agenda and circulate it to the participants. The agenda helps attendees prepare for the meeting's key topics, marshal their thoughts, and bring supporting documents or other evidence. (Those attendees who read the agenda, anyway.)

ChatGPT is skilled at creating logical and neatly laid out agendas. All you need to do is give it the necessary information:

- The meeting's name or purpose
- The attendees
- The topics the meeting will cover, in order
- How much time to schedule for each topic
- Which participants will lead which topics

The best time to create an agenda for the meeting is right after sending the invitation you had ChatGPT create for it. If you're still working in the same chat, ChatGPT knows most of the meeting's details, and you only need to add information about the allocation of topics and the allocation of time to those topics. Here's an example with the Budget Meeting for Next Year from the previous section:

> On that Budget Meeting for Next Year we just set up: Could you create an agenda for me? I'll start the meeting, welcome everyone, and state the purpose in five minutes. Jill's next: She'll speak for 15 minutes about budget parameters. We'll then have 30 minutes of questions and discussion. After that, I'll wrap up the meeting in 10 minutes.

From that prompt, ChatGPT drew up a tidy little agenda.

If the active chat doesn't have access to information about the meeting, you'll need to include all the information in the prompt. Here's an example:

> I'm having a meeting to discuss the move to the new office. I'll be chairing the meeting; the other people will be Bill, Larni, and Sue. Here's a list of the topics we need to cover: new office status, when it will be completed, how to reduce work for the transition, and the physical resources we'll need. Bill will talk about the status for 10 minutes, then we'll all discuss the other topics. The meeting should be an hour and a half max. Please write an agenda.

ChatGPT created a six-point agenda with a total time of 90 minutes.

If you realize you've gotten something wrong or left something off, simply ask ChatGPT to rewrite the agenda and add that item. Continuing the previous example, you might prompt ChatGPT like this:

> Add a new item before step 4 titled "Informing Staff About the Move." Make it 10 minutes long. Reduce the time for "Strategies to Reduce Workload During Transition" to 15 minutes.

Perform Meeting Preparation and Research

To get ready for the meeting, you may need to assemble background information. But why do the work yourself when you can have ChatGPT do it for you?

Here are a couple of examples:

 Can you give me a summary and explanation about inflation and its causes?

ChatGPT returned a short summary followed by a more detailed explanation.

Similarly, you could get ChatGPT to find information on a person with whom you'll be meeting:

 Please collect information on Tadhg Richardson of Choho Associates and give me a 200-word summary. Their office is in Santa Monica.

Organize and Structure Meeting Notes

After holding the meeting, you can have ChatGPT organize and structure the notes you took in it. Here are examples of prompts you might use:

 Here are my rough notes from the Budget Meeting for Next Year. Structure them into separate sections, each with a header and several bullet points.

After giving this prompt, you'd press Shift+Enter to create a line break, and then paste in the notes.

 We just had a brainstorming meeting and came up with some good ideas. I'd like you to organize the ideas into categories by theme.

Again, you'd paste in the notes after this prompt, putting a line break between the two.

> **TIP**   After holding a meeting on an online conferencing tool such as Zoom or Microsoft Teams, download the transcript from the meeting and have ChatGPT summarize it for you. Just give a command such as "Summarize the following notes," and then paste in the transcript.

If you often have meetings of the same type, you might save time and increase consistency by getting ChatGPT to create a template for notes from this type of meeting. For example, say you hold a weekly review meeting with each of your direct reports. You might give ChatGPT a prompt such as this:

Create a template for notes from my weekly review meetings with employees. The template should start with the date, followed by the employee's name and position. Then have sections for reviewing planned activities, checking in on progress with ongoing projects, identifying and discussing problems, and developing plans for upcoming projects.

ChatGPT created a neat template. I copied its contents into a new Word document and saved it as a template.

Follow Up After Meetings

To get the best results from your meeting, you'll likely need to follow up with the other participants on any action items decided in the meeting and on next steps planned.

Below are four examples of prompts you might use. The first three assume you're working in the chat that contains the notes ChatGPT structured for you in the previous section.

PROMPT You know those notes you just structured for me? I'd like you to create a summary of that meeting for me.

 PROMPT Working from those notes and the summary, make a list of four tasks we need to perform.

 PROMPT Still using those notes and that summary, recommend five reminders that might be beneficial.

If ChatGPT doesn't have the details of the meeting, you'll need to provide them. Here's an example of a prompt you might use:

 PROMPT Read the meeting transcript below and draft follow-up email messages. Write a separate email message for each meeting participant apart from me.

You'd then paste in the meeting transcript, probably after a line break (press Shift+Enter).

 Sure, I can help with that. Here are follow-up email drafts for each meeting participant based on the transcript:

Email to Bill

Subject: Follow-Up on Office Move Meeting and Your Next Steps

Dear Bill,

Thank you for your contribution to our recent meeting about the office move. . . .

Manage Your Email Efficiently

Email began as a boon, but these days, it tends to be more of a bane for many knowledge workers. If you've ever spent hours trying to reach the bottom of an inbox that keeps filling up with fresh messages; if you find yourself constantly having to delete junk, spam, and newsletters; or if you get stuck phrasing awkward messages, you should enlist ChatGPT's assistance.

How Can ChatGPT Help with Your Email?

Chances are you'd like to be able to hand over your work inbox to ChatGPT with a terse command such as "Deal with this for me."

Sadly, that's not in the cards — at least not yet. As of this writing, you cannot set up ChatGPT to access your email directly, either in an email client app (such as Windows Mail or Apple Mail) or in an online email implementation (such as by giving ChatGPT the credentials for your Gmail account or your Outlook.com account). The limitations are in place to protect your data from possible damage or loss.

Because of these limitations, ChatGPT can help you only in ways such as the following:

- Giving you advice on prioritizing email, minimizing spam, organizing your message folders, and so on.
- Summarizing or otherwise manipulating messages you share with ChatGPT by pasting them into the Send a Message box.
- Drafting email messages for you. You then copy the draft, paste it into your email client, and address and send the message manually.

Get Advice on Working with Email

To get ChatGPT's advice on how to work with email, use prompts such as the following:

(PROMPT) **Tell me how to prioritize my incoming email messages.**

ChatGPT suggested identifying key contacts as VIPs, which directs their messages to a special inbox; using email filters to identify important and unimportant messages and move them to suitable folders; and starring or flagging vital messages for later attention to prevent them from getting submerged in the e-maelstrom.

(PROMPT) **How do I create a rule in Apple Mail?**

ChatGPT spelled out the steps to create a rule.

(PROMPT) **Tell me three ways to save time and effort in Windows Mail.**

ChatGPT recommended pinning your most-used email addresses to the Start menu for immediate access, creating a unified inbox that enables you to view messages from multiple accounts in a single place, and setting up personalized notifications for your key email accounts.

(PROMPT) **How can I create a folder in Gmail?**

ChatGPT explained that Gmail uses labels rather than folders, and gave straightforward instructions for creating a label.

Have ChatGPT Summarize or Otherwise Manipulate a Message

If you want to have ChatGPT work on a message you have received, you need to do it the hard way: Open the message, copy its contents, and paste the contents into the Send a Message box along with a suitable prompt. Here are three examples:

 Summarize the following message in 50 words.

 Read the following newsletter, identify the three most important points, and write a short bulleted paragraph about each.

PROMPT **Read the following message and draft a reply for me.**

If the draft hits the spot, copy it and paste it into a reply in your email client, and then send the message manually. If the draft isn't what you need, tell ChatGPT how to improve it.

Have ChatGPT Draft a New Message for You

As well as drafting the reply to a message, ChatGPT is happy to draft new messages for you. Just tell ChatGPT what you need. Here are two examples:

Draft email messages to Liz Jones and Ralph Martinez reminding them that the deadline for newsletter submissions is 5 p.m. on Monday. Remind Liz that she committed to submitting the schedule for the Austin project. Remind Ralph that he still needs to meet with me to finalize his deliverable.

Subject: Reminder: Deadline for Newsletter Submissions - Monday at 5 p.m.

Dear Liz,

I hope this message finds you well. I wanted to remind you about the upcoming deadline for our newsletter submissions, which is due by 5 p.m. on Monday.

As discussed in our last team meeting, you committed to submitting the schedule for the Austin project. . . .

PROMPT **Help me write an email to my son's teacher apologizing for him not handing in his homework last Friday. I know this sounds like a joke, but our dog actually ate his homework. My son's name is Danny. The dog is Max.**

ChatGPT did a lovely job with this unpromising prompt. (It included this sentence: "Danny had completed the assignment and left it on the kitchen table, but Max, being the playful pup he is, thought it was a new toy.")

Follow up with other prompts as needed until ChatGPT has whipped each draft into the shape you need. Then copy the text, paste each draft into a new message in your email client, and address and send the message manually.

Plan and Arrange Travel

As of this writing, ChatGPT cannot arrange travel for you, but it can help you pick out the flights and hotels you want. ChatGPT can also give you advice on everything from minimizing jet lag to avoiding problems caused by misunderstanding local customs.

Search for Flights and Hotels

To search for flights and hotels, you need to activate ChatGPT's Plugins Model and load one or more plug-ins that connect ChatGPT to travel services. Follow these steps:

1. Click the New Chat button at the top of the sidebar to start a new chat.

2. Click the GPT-4 tab to make it active.

3. Move the pointer over the GPT-4 tab button without clicking. The pop-up panel appears.

4. Click the Plugins button, so that the blue check mark appears on it. The icons for the currently active plug-ins appear below the GPT-3.5 and GPT-4 tabs.

5. If you can tell from the icons that appear that you've got the right plug-ins loaded, you're all set. If not, click the drop-down arrow to display the list of plug-ins, and then select the check box for each plug-in you want to use.

ChatGPT Plug-Ins for Searching for Flights and Hotels

As of this writing, various plug-ins are available that enable ChatGPT to search for flights. These plug-ins include Skyscanner, JetBook.click, Trip.com, KAYAK, and Expedia.

Similarly, the Plugin Store offers assorted plug-ins that enable ChatGPT to search for hotels. These plug-ins include Travelmyth, Trip.com (hello again!), and Vio.com.

If you need to install plug-ins, click the drop-down arrow to the right of the plug-in icons to display the list of plug-ins, and then click the Plugin Store button at the bottom of the list to open the Plugin Store dialog box. Browse or search for the plug-ins you need. When you find a plug-in you want, click its Install button.

When you've installed all the plug-ins you want, click the Close (X) button to close the Plugin Store dialog box. You can then enable and disable plug-ins by selecting or clearing their check boxes in the list of plug-ins.

There are two complications. First, as of this writing, ChatGPT allows you to load only a maximum of three plug-ins in a chat; so choose wisely, Grasshopper. (You can start another chat and load different plug-ins in it.) Second, some plug-ins are mutually exclusive, and you can enable only one at a time. For example, the Expedia plug-in and the KAYAK plug-in won't work together. If you try to enable both, you'll see a message such as *You can't enable Expedia while KAYAK is enabled.* So if you run into this problem, you'll need to decide which of the two plug-ins to use.

Once you've chosen your plug-ins, go ahead and prompt ChatGPT to start searching for what you want. Here are examples of prompts:

Can you find me a flight from Houston to LAX after 4 p.m. today?

ChatGPT used KAYAK and returned a list of five flights, including the airline, the departure time, the arrival time, the number of stops, and the price. Each item had a Book Here link leading to a page on Kayak.com where I could book the flight.

 Can you find me an inexpensive hotel in Paris, France, for the nights of August 20 and 21?

ChatGPT used Travelmyth and came back with three budget hotels, all of which claimed to be dog-friendly.

 Thanks. I can afford a bit more than that. Please find a hotel in Paris for those dates costing around $100 per night. And not dog-friendly, please.

ChatGPT switched to KAYAK and came back with three hotels around my target price.

 Can you work out an itinerary for me? I need to fly from Chicago to Berlin for a meeting next Wednesday. Then fly on to Madrid for a meeting on Friday morning. Then fly back to Chicago on Saturday or Sunday. Find me flights and four-star hotels.

ChatGPT used KAYAK and put together a complete itinerary that was (forgive me) just the ticket, including a booking link for each flight and each hotel.

Get Travel Advice

Once you've nailed down your itinerary, you can ask ChatGPT for travel advice. Here are three examples:

 I'm going on a ten-day trip to Europe in August. Mostly business, but I'll have some free time for tourism. Draw up a packing list for me.

ChatGPT returned a comprehensive list, broken up into sections for Documents, Clothing, Electronics, Toiletries, and Miscellaneous.

 For one night in France, I have the choice between staying in Béziers and staying in Perpignan. Which do you recommend, and why?

ChatGPT emphasized that the choice of city depended on me and my interests. It gave a brief description of each city and concluded:

 If you are interested in history and prefer a quieter, smaller city, Béziers might be a good choice for you. However, if you enjoy a more vibrant atmosphere with a mix of cultures and more entertainment options, Perpignan would be more suitable.

 How can I minimize jet lag? Is traveling east worse for jet lag than traveling west?

ChatGPT told me that jet lag is also known as *desynchronosis* (that's your new word for today) and gave me six standard tips for minimizing it. ChatGPT said traveling east might be harder on our body clocks than traveling west but advised me not to plan my travel based solely on this consideration. (As if!)

ChatGPT Prompts for Business Writing

IF YOUR WORK includes creating any type of business documents, make sure you take advantage of ChatGPT's capabilities to save yourself time and effort. ChatGPT can create a wide range of business documents — everything from short memos and business letters all the way through to business plans and long-form sales letters.

In this chapter, we'll look at prompts you can give ChatGPT to write copy for ads, social media, and other uses; prompts to write proposals; and prompts to write business letters. At the end of the chapter, we'll examine prompts for getting ChatGPT to edit and proofread your work.

As when working with an assistant or a colleague, you should carefully review the material ChatGPT provides for you before using it. In many cases, you'll want to tweak the material further to personalize it or to make it express exactly what you need.

Two types of business documents we *won't* cover in this chapter are resumes and web pages (see Chapters 2 and 7, respectively).

To make sure we're on the same (virtual) page from the start, we'll begin by looking at how you work with ChatGPT on creating documents.

Understand How You Work on Documents with ChatGPT

As you saw in Chapters 2 and 3, ChatGPT doesn't have access to your computer's file system as of this writing, so it cannot create new document files or work with your existing files. Similarly, ChatGPT cannot log in to your online accounts, such as your Microsoft 365 account or your Dropbox account, so it cannot create or access files in those online accounts, either. ChatGPT is confined to your web browser or to the ChatGPT app on your iPhone, iPad, or Android device.

This limitation helps protect you and your data by preventing ChatGPT from taking unauthorized or unwise actions in your computer's file system or your online accounts. That's sensible, given the potential for damage, but it means that when you're working with ChatGPT, you're the one who must perform any document creation or manipulation. When you're using ChatGPT to create a new document, ChatGPT can supply the content, but you have to copy that content to a file and save the file. When you want ChatGPT to work on an existing file, you must copy that file's content and paste it into the Send a Message box to pass it to ChatGPT. If ChatGPT's work with the file produces output you want to save, you'll need to copy the output and paste it into a file.

Enter Text Quickly Using Dictation

The standard way to enter text in the Send a Message box is by typing it, but you can also dictate text. Dictation is especially useful in the ChatGPT app, both because dictating is so much faster than using the onscreen keyboards and because you can dictate without having to look at the screen, using either your device's built-in microphone or a headset. For example, you can enter text via dictation on your iPhone while walking, driving (local laws permitting), or performing other activities. Dictation can also be a great help if you suffer from dyslexia, dyspraxia, or a similar disorder.

Better yet, you can have ChatGPT edit and proof the material you dictate. So if you find that giving punctuation commands spoils the flow of your dictation, skip the punctuation and let ChatGPT add it for you afterward. As usual, you'll want to check ChatGPT's changes before using the text.

Write Copy

If your job involves creating copy, you should enlist ChatGPT's help to create it more quickly and with less effort. And if your job involves commissioning others to write copy, you should see how much of that copy ChatGPT can produce and how much you still need to assign to human copywriters.

NOTE "Copy" in this sense means text created for advertising or other marketing communications. Copy aims to persuade the reader or listener to take a specific action, such as buying the product the copy is advertising.

Whether you're looking for advertising copywriting, content copywriting, direct-response copywriting, or social-media copywriting, ChatGPT is happy to help. Simply prompt ChatGPT with details of what you need, as in the following examples:

 Please write a memorable slogan for our new product, a pencil that sticks to your car's windshield so it's always on hand.

 "Always Write, Right in Sight — The Pencil That's Miles Ahead!"

Hey, could you whip up a quick script for a 15-second radio ad offering all-you-can-eat donuts while you get your car's tires changed?

ChatGPT delivered a script that started like this and included suggestions for sound effects:

 [SFX: Car tires screeching, transition to upbeat music.]

Narrator: (Excited) "Get your tires changed and enjoy a sweet treat! At Bob's Auto Service, it's All-You-Can-Eat Donuts, while you wait!"

 Please give me a snappy headline for an online advert offering five free washes when you join the Laundromat Society.

 "Wash, Rinse, and Repeat! Sign Up for the Laundromat Society and Enjoy Five Washes on Us!"

 Okay, Chatsworth, draft me a blog post about how 20 minutes of deep breathing straight after you get out of bed puts you in a good mood for the day.

 Sure, here's a draft blog post on that topic:

Title: *Energize Your Mornings: Deep Breathing for a Brighter Day*

ChatGPT delivered a short but targeted blog post suitable for use with only the smallest of tweaks. (By the way, ChatGPT raised no objection to my use of a pet name for it in this example. So if you want to use a friendly name, go right ahead.)

I'd like you to write a 1,000-word direct-response article for our new product, Pitcairn Manuka. This is the ultimate in blended honeys. It combines the health benefits of Manuka honey with the sought-after taste of Pitcairn honey. This honey is special because it is available only in limited quantities, so we are selling it only via yearly subscriptions.

ChatGPT did a terrific job of selling this imaginary product. I was particularly impressed by the following section, which managed to spin the prompt's entirely bogus rationale for the subscription model into a positive feature.

The Exclusivity of Subscription

Pitcairn Manuka is not just honey. It's a luxury, a sensory journey, a wellness tool. Its production is meticulously overseen to ensure the highest quality, leading to limited availability.

To guarantee your share of this exclusive product, we're offering Pitcairn Manuka through yearly subscriptions only. Subscribers will receive their allotment of Pitcairn Manuka throughout the year, ensuring they have continuous access to this remarkable honey blend.

Are you tempted? I was!

Write Proposals

ChatGPT can help you to write various types of business proposals — anything from a business plan proposal or an investment proposal to a research proposal or a grant proposal.

To get started, tell ChatGPT the type of proposal you want and what you're proposing. Provide as many details as possible, such as a timeline, the people or bodies involved, the budget, and so on.

Write a Project Proposal

Here is a prompt you might give to get ChatGPT to draft a project proposal:

 Help me put together a project proposal for a nonprofit organization that's going to launch an evening program for kids in the community whose parents work nights and can't look after them. The program will provide supervised evening activities, all age-appropriate, in a safe location and run by accredited volunteers. It'll take us about five months to get started. Could you write a draft proposal for me?

ChatGPT came back with a neatly structured proposal that started like this:

 Title: Proposal for Community Evening Program for Children

Executive Summary:

This proposal is put forth by [Your Name/Your Organization's Name] to launch a community evening program aimed at supporting families in our community where parents work night shifts . . .

Write a Business Plan Proposal

Here is a prompt you could give to ask ChatGPT to write a business plan proposal for you:

 Hi again. I'd like you to write a business plan proposal for me. The business is to help companies and organizations dispose of their old and broken tech items responsibly instead of keeping them forever or just junking them.

Our technicians will go into offices and collect the old items. We'll then repair or recondition any items worth using and recycle any items not worth using. I need the business plan to persuade potential investors to back me. Could you draw up a draft proposal for this business plan?

Title: Business Plan Proposal for Responsible Tech Disposal and Recycling Services

Executive Summary:

Our venture seeks to address a growing need in the tech industry – the responsible and efficient disposal of outdated and broken tech items. We will offer a service to companies and organizations to collect, repair, recondition, and recycle their old tech items, thereby reducing environmental impact and promoting a circular economy. . . .

Write a Research Proposal

When you need to put together a research proposal, you might enlist ChatGPT's help by using a prompt such as this:

PROMPT **Hey, ChatGPT, can you write me a research proposal? It's for my thesis. The topic is Use of Artificial Sweeteners in Commercial Catering. I'll be gathering data via questionnaires and field observations. I'll be doing six months of research.**

ChatGPT wrote a detailed proposal titled "Use of Artificial Sweeteners in Commercial Catering: A Quantitative Investigation" that ran from "I. Introduction and Background" to "VI: Expected Outcomes and Conclusions."

Write a Grant Proposal

If you need to create a grant proposal, ChatGPT has you covered. All you need to do is prompt ChatGPT with the necessary information — for example:

Create a grant proposal for me. I'm looking to get funding to start a traditional music group for teenagers. The group will keep teenagers out of trouble on Saturday afternoons, encourage them to learn to play acoustic instruments, and preserve traditional music from being lost by bringing it live to modern audiences.

ChatGPT created a detailed proposal that started like this:

Title: Preserving Traditions: Engaging Youth through Traditional Music

I. Executive Summary

The goal of our initiative, "Preserving Traditions," is to engage teenagers in productive activities during their free time while preserving our cultural heritage through traditional music. This project aims to establish a traditional music group that will encourage teenagers to learn and play acoustic instruments, instill a sense of discipline, and allow them to share their talents with contemporary audiences.

Write Business Letters

ChatGPT is great at writing all kinds of business letters, from invitation letters to proposal letters, and from job-offer letters to resignation and termination letters. You just need to tell ChatGPT what kind of letter you need and then provide as much of the necessary information as possible. If ChatGPT is missing a vital piece of information, it leaves a placeholder for you to fill in.

Here's an example of asking ChatGPT to write a letter recommending someone for a job:

Draft a letter of recommendation for Xuan Murphy. She's a Team Supervisor at this company and reports directly to me. She's been here for five years and has had three promotions, taking on more responsibility each time. Her notable strengths are communication, time management, and project tracking. She's applying for a Project Manager job with the Arctic Research Commission.

Because I didn't provide the recipient's name, ChatGPT addressed the letter "To whom it may concern." The rest of the letter was well written, needing only minor adjustments. In particular, look at the detail that ChatGPT summoned up to illustrate my mention of Xuan's notable strength in project tracking:

Perhaps her most commendable strength is her proficiency in project tracking. Xuan has developed a systematic and efficient approach to monitoring project milestones and tracking progress. Her scrupulous eye for detail, combined with her understanding of big-picture project goals, allows her to anticipate challenges, adjust plans as needed, and ensure projects are completed on time and to the highest standards.

Here's an example of prompting ChatGPT to write a payment reminder letter:

Hey, ChatGPT, could you write me a payment reminder letter for an unpaid invoice? The amount due is $3,500 for office supplies. The client is Goldbrick Pharmaceuticals. The payment is 60 days overdue, so this is the final reminder. Be polite but firm, okay?

When you finally reach the limit of your patience with your employer, prompt ChatGPT to write your letter of resignation. Here's an example:

Write me a resignation letter, would you? I'm sick of my employer paying me weeks late and making me work overtime without notice or compensation. Fifteen days' notice from today. Make the letter formal but let them know I'm unhappy.

ChatGPT handled this request well, writing a commendably formal letter that made the employee's dissatisfactions clear. Here's an excerpt:

While I appreciate the demanding nature of our industry, the consistent delay in payment of salary and the regular requirement for uncompensated overtime have significantly affected my professional satisfaction and personal life. As a committed professional, I respect the necessity for occasional extra hours, but the frequency of these expectations, combined with the issues with my remuneration, have resulted in an unsustainable situation.

On the other side of the coin, you can have ChatGPT handle the awkward task of writing a termination letter for you.

I'd like you to write a formal termination letter for Mary Peterson, our Executive Assistant in this department. Mary is on the final month of her three-month probation and has not come to grips with her duties despite three warnings and two performance improvement plans. Her employment will terminate at the end of next week. We wish her all the best in her search for a suitable position, etc., etc.

ChatGPT produced a suitably formal termination letter, including details of when Mary will get her final paycheck and how she should return any company property before leaving the premises. (You'll notice my prompt didn't mention company property; ChatGPT included that as one of the components of a standard dismissal letter. As always, you should check ChatGPT's work closely and make any necessary changes before using it.)

> **NOTE**   Because of the sensitivity of exit and termination pro-
> cedures, ChatGPT recommended having both the resignation
> letter and the termination letter reviewed by a legal professional
> or an HR expert.

Edit and Proofread Your Work

Having ChatGPT write text for you is great, but there will likely be
times when you want to do the writing yourself. In such cases, you may
want to have ChatGPT edit and proofread what you've written.

"Edit and proofread"? What are the differences between the two?

Glad you asked. Here are the types of checking you can ask
ChatGPT to do and what each involves:

- **Proofread.** ChatGPT checks for misspellings, punctuation problems, and basic grammatical errors.
- **Copyedit.** ChatGPT checks the text's style, consistency, and
  word usage, correcting obvious issues, pointing out potentially
  better word choices, and suggesting improvements to sentence
  structure.
- **Content edit.** ChatGPT examines the text's overall structure,
  content, and style, and assesses its clarity and readability. Where
  ChatGPT detects potential problems, it suggests improvements.
- **Resume edit.** ChatGPT is great at resumes — creating them,
  editing them, proofing them, and more. See Chapter 2 for more
  information.
- **Academic edit.** ChatGPT can analyze academic texts, such as
  essays or research papers, for structure and clarity, and can suggest improvements.
- **Developmental edit.** ChatGPT can read your early draft of a
  manuscript; assess the content, style, structure, and pacing; and
  suggest improvements. Developmental editing is sometimes
  called *substantive editing* and usually takes place early in the
  development of the manuscript.

Here are four examples of prompts you could use for editing and proofing. For each of them, you would paste in the text after the prompt and a line break (press Shift+Enter).

 Proofread the following article and identify any spelling errors, punctuation problems, or grammar issues.

 I'd like you to copyedit this blog post and point out any structure issues. If any word choices seem poor, recommend better choices.

 Edit the white paper (text below) for content and clarity. Make sure the ideas flow logically. Suggest improvements for any issues.

 Hiya! Here's the plot for a short story. Read through it as a developmental editor would and tell me ways to make it more compelling.

What Can a Human Editor Offer That ChatGPT Doesn't?

The range of different types of editing that ChatGPT can perform is highly impressive, as are ChatGPT's language skills in general. But to what extent should you rely on ChatGPT's editing, and should you ever involve a human editor? The answers to those questions vary depending on the type of text you're creating and how important the purpose for which you're planning to use it is.

ChatGPT is very strong on proofreading. It nails misspellings and basic grammatical errors with aplomb and identifies suitable fixes for most punctuation problems.

ChatGPT is also very good at copyediting. Most of its criticisms are accurate and its fixes are suitable, even though you might decide not to implement them all.

Beyond that, ChatGPT is terrific at reading, writing, and reconfiguring resumes, as noted above.

For more advanced types of editing, such as content editing and developmental editing, ChatGPT is not as strong — and it is willing to admit as much. When I asked about content editing, ChatGPT warned me that "my capabilities in this area may be limited since nuanced understanding of content often requires human judgement."

If your work needs content editing or developmental editing, by all means try ChatGPT first. But if you're not confident that ChatGPT's suggestions will give your work the focus or the quality it needs, you should probably involve a human editor. A human editor can also add value by editing a work to give it a particular style, such as a company's business style or a publisher's house style, or to develop or enhance a vision the author is trying to express through the work.

5

ChatGPT Prompts for Research and Analysis

IF YOU PERFORM research as part of your work or your studies, you can harness ChatGPT's power to complete that research more quickly. In this chapter, we'll look at how to prompt ChatGPT to summarize articles you might want to read, analyze data you've captured, and suggest topics connected to the topics you're researching. We'll also cover how to prompt ChatGPT to generate research questions for you and how to enlist ChatGPT's help to design experiments.

Ready?

Summarize Articles

If you had infinite time, you could read all the literature on the subject you need to study or to understand. But as your time is limited, you may want to get ChatGPT to summarize one or more articles for you. This can be a great way to get a quick overview of an article — enough, at least, to determine whether you should read the article yourself.

> **WARNING**   As of this writing, ChatGPT seems to have a hard time identifying satire, irony, and sarcasm. ChatGPT's summary of an article that includes these elements may make the article sound serious.

If you enable the Web Browsing Model, ChatGPT can summarize articles on the web, provided they are not hidden behind paywalls or otherwise restricted. Give a prompt like this:

PROMPT   **Summarize URL**

ChatGPT reads the article and returns a summary.

Without the Web Browsing Model enabled, you must paste into the Send a Message box the content you want ChatGPT to summarize. Give the "Summarize" prompt, paste the material, and press Enter.

PROMPT   **Summarize *pasted_material***

This method works fine, and is usually quicker than having ChatGPT access the material on the web, but it means that the content can be only up to 4096 tokens long (including the "Summarize" keyword), so you cannot summarize longer articles.

Leaving the "Summarize" prompt open like this lets ChatGPT decide on the length of summary to create. Results vary depending on how long the article is and what its contents are, but ChatGPT typically delivers an introductory paragraph, a number of key points, and a concluding paragraph.

If you want ChatGPT to keep the summary to a certain length, give the limit. For example:

PROMPT   **Summarize in 50 words URL**

Alternatively, you might ask for a specific number of key points. For example:

(PROMPT) **Summarize in three key points URL**

Analyze Data

ChatGPT can help you to analyze data you have captured. ChatGPT can perform various types of analysis, including these five types:

- **Descriptive analysis.** This simple form of analysis provides a basic understanding of the data by calculating simple metrics, such as the mean, median, mode, and standard deviation.
- **Correlation analysis.** This type of analysis enables you to determine if there's a correlation between two variables. (Spoiler: Correlation does not prove causation.)
- **Regression analysis.** This more sophisticated form of correlation analysis tries to show how one variable is affected by one or more other variables.
- **Time series analysis.** This form of analysis helps you understand trends and seasonality in data collected over an extended period of time.
- **Sentiment analysis.** This form of analysis examines the sentiment expressed in text — for example, in a customer review of a product.

Here are three examples of prompts you could use to ask ChatGPT to analyze data. For each prompt, you would give the data to ChatGPT by pasting it into the Send a Message box after the prompt and (optionally) a line break (press Shift+Enter).

 Could you analyze the following data and tell me the mean, the median, the mode, the variance, and the standard deviation?

ChatGPT spelled out the meaning of the five measures, demonstrated how to work out each of them, and then provided this summary:

So, for this data set:

- *Mean = 57.14*
- *Median = 60*
- *Mode = 80*
- *Variance = 420.33*
- *Standard Deviation = 20.50*

Here's some data from a survey we did that shows the length of customer service calls in seconds and the customer satisfaction rating on a scale of 1 (worst) to 10 (best). Have a look at them and tell me if there's a correlation between the two.

The data you've provided seems to suggest a positive correlation between the length of customer service calls and the customer satisfaction rating. This is because as the length of the call increases, the customer satisfaction rating also increases.

However, to accurately determine the correlation, you would typically calculate the Pearson correlation coefficient. . . .

ChatGPT explained that it doesn't currently have the capability to calculate mathematical or statistical functions. It suggested using a programming language, such as R or Python, to perform the calculation — and provided a complete Python script for calculating the correlation coefficient.

Hi ChatGPT! I'm giving you ten customer reviews for our new chewable mouse mat. Do a quick sentiment analysis on them, would you?

ChatGPT analyzed each of the customer reviews, determining whether it expressed positive sentiment, negative sentiment, neutral sentiment, or mixed sentiment. Here are three examples:

1. ***"This product is useless, but it made me laugh."*** - *Mixed sentiment. Negative due to "useless" but also positive because it made the customer laugh.*

4. ***"Fun for 5-year-olds."*** - *Positive sentiment. "Fun" indicates enjoyment or amusement.*

10. ***"This may be chewable, but the flavor is disgusting."*** - *Negative sentiment. "Disgusting" is a strong negative word.*

Reducing text to a value (such as "negative sentiment") feels somewhat grotesque, but greatly simplifies the task of analyzing complex input. ChatGPT does warn that automated tools "may not always interpret sentiment accurately, especially when it comes to sarcasm, irony, or culturally specific expression"; keep this in mind if you use sentiment analysis.

Suggest Connected Topics

If you need to look into topics connected to what you are studying, you can ask ChatGPT for help in identifying them. Here are three examples of prompts you could use:

 I'm examining the positive and negative effects of social media usage during the pandemic. Please suggest three connected topics for me to look at.

ChatGPT suggested Mental Health and Social Media, Social Media as a Source of Information and Misinformation, and Social Media and Physical Activity.

 Hey, ChatGPT, I'm studying the effect of daytime napping on academic performance in college students. Could you give me five related topics to consider?

ChatGPT suggested topics including Sleep Deprivation and Cognitive Function, Impact of Stress on Sleep Quality, and the Role of Circadian Rhythms in Sleep and Academic Performance.

 I'm working on the effect that reducing the serving size of fast-food takeout dishes will have on the rat population of major urban areas. Give me 10 connected topics I should think about. Thanks!

 Certainly, your topic is an interesting intersection of public health, urban ecology, and behavioral science. Here are ten related topics that you might consider:

ChatGPT's suggested topics included Urban Waste Management, Rat Behavior and Diet, Impact of Fast-Food Industry on Urban Ecosystems, and Fast-Food Consumption Trends.

Generate Research Questions

ChatGPT can be a valuable resource when you need to generate research questions to probe an area of interest. Instead of you having to cudgel your brains to produce the questions, you can have ChatGPT suggest them in seconds from its vast reading and data banks.

Start by telling ChatGPT the topic in which you're interested and identifying the gaps in current knowledge. Here's an example:

 We know that exercise affects appetite. I want to research how the intensity of exercise changes the effect on appetite. For example, some people report being ravenously hungry after intense exercise, whereas other people don't want to eat at all for several hours after intense exercise. Can you generate some research questions for me on this subject?

ChatGPT returned seven potential research questions, including these three:

Is there a correlation between the intensity of exercise and the types of food (e.g., protein, carbohydrates, fat) that individuals crave post-exercise?

How does intense exercise influence the physiological hunger and satiety hormones (like ghrelin and leptin) compared to moderate or light exercise?

Is there a difference in post-exercise appetite between aerobic exercises (like running) and anaerobic exercises (like weightlifting) of similar intensity?

Here's another example:

I'm investigating the roles of different activities in the acquisition of a foreign language. I want to compare the helpfulness of spoken role-play, in-class group exercises (also spoken), and written exercises. Which activities help students learn most quickly? Please generate eight research questions I could use.

ChatGPT returned the eight questions I requested, including these three:

How does the complexity level of the target language affect the effectiveness of spoken role-play, in-class group exercises, and written exercises?

How does student engagement and motivation change with each of the three activities (spoken role-play, in-class group exercises, and written exercises) and how does this influence language acquisition speed?

Which of the three activities (spoken role-play, in-class group exercises, or written exercises) contributes more effectively to long-term retention of a foreign language?

Design Experiments

ChatGPT can help you to design experiments that you can perform to further your research. Normally, you'd start off with a research question — for example, a question that your instructor has given you.

Understand the 10 Steps in Designing an Experiment

Designing an experiment typically involves the following 10 steps:

1. Defining the experiment's objective.
2. Developing a hypothesis that predicts the experiment's outcomes.
3. Designing a methodology that suits your research question.
4. Identifying the experiment's independent variables, dependent variables, and controlled variables.
5. Deciding how to collect data for the experiment.
6. Choosing a suitable sample size and appropriate selection techniques.
7. Selecting suitable analysis methods to analyze the data collected.
8. Assessing any ethical considerations involved in the experiment.
9. Identifying any potential sources of error in the experiment.
10. Reporting the results of your experiment.

We'll now work through those 10 steps explained in the previous section. We'll use this research question:

For overweight and obese adults, does a low-carbohydrate diet improve weight-loss outcomes compared to a standard American diet?

1. Define the Objective

Let's start by defining the objective. You might prompt like this:

 I need to design an experiment for the following research question. First, please help me to define the objective of the experiment.

After the prompts, you'd press Shift+Enter to insert a line break, and then press Ctrl+V to paste in the objective.

ChatGPT returned the objective with some suggestions:

 The objective of your experiment, based on your research question, would be:

"To compare the effectiveness of a low-carbohydrate diet versus a standard American diet on weight-loss outcomes in overweight and obese adults."

To further refine your objectives, you may want to define what specific weight-loss outcomes you're interested in. For example:

- *Total weight loss after a certain period (e.g., 3 months, 6 months).*
- *Changes in body mass index (BMI).*
- *Changes in body fat percentage.*
- *Long-term maintenance of weight loss (e.g., after 1 year).*

2. Develop a Hypothesis

Next, we need to develop a hypothesis that predicts the experiment's outcomes. We can use a prompt such as this:

 Please suggest a hypothesis based on that objective.

ChatGPT suggested the following hypothesis:

"Overweight and obese adults following a low-carbohydrate diet will experience greater weight loss outcomes compared to those following a standard American diet over a defined period."

ChatGPT also suggested using a specific measure for assessing the weight-loss outcomes, such as total weight loss, decrease in BMI, or decrease in body-fat percentage. So I prompted:

 That hypothesis is good, but please add "total weight loss" as the measure.

ChatGPT made that change.

3. Design a Methodology for the Experiment

The next step is to design a methodology that suits the research question. We can prompt ChatGPT like this:

PROMPT **Design a methodology for the experiment.**

ChatGPT explained that we need to design a controlled experiment — one that has a control group that will enable us to tell whether our intervention has worked. We will recruit enough overweight and obese adults to make a sample, explaining the experiment to them and making sure they understand the purpose and the risks. We then assign the subjects randomly to the intervention group and the control group, perform the intervention for our determined period, and measure the results.

4. Identify the Independent, Dependent, and Controlled Variables

Next, we need to identify the experiment's independent variables, dependent variables, and controlled variables. ChatGPT can spell these out:

> (PROMPT) **What are the experiment's independent variables, dependent variables, and controlled variables?**

ChatGPT explained that the independent variable is the one we manipulate: the participants' type of diet. The dependent variable is the variable we measure: the participants' weight. The controlled variables are variables we keep the same for all participants, such as their total caloric intake, activity levels, and frequency of weight measurement.

5. Decide How to Collect Data

The next step is to decide how to collect data for the experiment. I prompted ChatGPT like this:

> (PROMPT) **How should I collect data for the experiment?**

ChatGPT explained that the experiment needs at least the weight, but other measurements may be useful, too. We may want to measure height so we can calculate BMI, measure body fat percentage, or measure other health indicators.

ChatGPT walked me through initial data collection, ongoing data collection at regular intervals during the study period, and final data collection at the end of the study.

6. Choose the Sample Size and Selection Techniques

Next, you need to choose a suitable sample size and appropriate selection techniques for the study. I prompted ChatGPT like this:

> (PROMPT) **What sample size and selection techniques should I use for the experiment?**

ChatGPT explained that the larger the sample size, the more closely it will represent the population and the greater its statistical significance will be — but that I also need to work within my resources. ChatGPT mentioned that I could run a power analysis to calculate the appropriate sample size.

Similarly, ChatGPT pointed out that, while random selection of participants would give a truer representation of the population, convenience sampling (in lay terms, taking whatever participants you can get) is likely to be more practical.

7. Select Suitable Analysis Methods

The seventh step is to select suitable analysis methods to analyze the data collected. I prompted ChatGPT for advice like this:

> (PROMPT) **What analysis methods should I use to analyze the data collected in the experiment?**

ChatGPT recommended calculating descriptive statistics for the intervention group and the control group, such as calculating the mean and the medium to measure the central tendency of the weight loss and calculating the range and the standard deviation to measure its dispersion. Next, ChatGPT suggested moving on to inferential statistics and using a t-test if the data meets the assumptions for parametric tests, or using a non-parametric test, such as the Mann-Whitney U test, if it does not.

If I collected data on confounding variables, I could use multivariate regression or analysis of covariance (ANCOVA) to control for them.

Whatever the other results, I should calculate the effect size to measure the size of the difference between the control group and the intervention group.

8. Assess Any Ethical Considerations

Next, I should assess any ethical considerations involved in the experiment. To this end, I prompted ChatGPT thus:

(PROMPT) Please assess any ethical considerations involved in the experiment.

ChatGPT produced a comprehensive list, starting with Informed Consent and Confidentiality and ending with Fair Participant Selection, Ethics Committee Approval, and Scientific Integrity.

9. Identify Potential Sources of Error

Next, I need to identify potential sources of error in the experiment:

(PROMPT) Identify any potential sources of error in the experiment.

ChatGPT returned a list of potential sources of error, such as dietary adherence, physical activity levels, measurement errors, and confounding variables (such as sleep patterns, stress levels, or genetic factors).

10. Report the Results

All that remains is to report the results of the experiment. ChatGPT is happy to provide advice on how to do this. I prompted:

(PROMPT) How can I report the results of the experiment?

ChatGPT recommended presenting the findings, methods, and results in the form of a scientific research paper, which would have these sections:

- Title
- Abstract
- Introduction
- Methods
- Results
- Discussion
- Conclusions
- References

ChatGPT Prompts for Communication and Knowledge Sharing

IN THIS CHAPTER, we'll look at how you can use ChatGPT to facilitate communication with your colleagues and streamline the sharing of knowledge with them. First, we'll cover prompts for facilitating communication by using ChatGPT to draft email messages and responses, check the tone of a message or a document and change it if necessary, translate communications from one language to another, and practice conversations. After that, we'll move on to prompts for streamlining knowledge sharing by using ChatGPT for actions such as generating documents to share, creating training materials, and brainstorming ideas and solutions.

Facilitate Communication

ChatGPT can facilitate communication between you and your colleagues in four main ways that we'll examine here. First, you can use ChatGPT to draft new email messages and responses to messages you've received. Second, you can ask ChatGPT to check the tone of a message or a document — and then rewrite it to change the tone if necessary. Third, you can get ChatGPT to translate a communication from one language to another, enabling you and people who use other languages to communicate more confidently with each other.

Fourth, you can use ChatGPT to practice important conversations before you hold them; the practice is necessarily written rather than spoken, but it can still be helpful.

The following subsections cover each of these actions in turn.

Use ChatGPT to Draft New Emails and Responses

Having ChatGPT draft new email messages and write responses to incoming messages can save you a huge amount of time and effort. We've visited this subject several times already in this book, especially in Chapter 3, which discusses managing your work and schedule, so we'll touch on it only lightly here.

To have ChatGPT draft a new email for you, prompt ChatGPT with what you need. Here's an example:

Write an email message to Joanna Diaz in HR. Address her as "Jo." Ask her when she will get the job advertisement for the Marketing Assistant position to me for approval. Tell her I'll be out of the office and unreachable next week.

ChatGPT returned a straightforward message that started like this:

Subject: Marketing Assistant Position Job Advertisement

Dear Jo,

I hope this email finds you well.

I'm reaching out regarding the job advertisement for the Marketing Assistant position. Could you please let me know when I might expect to receive it for approval?

I also wanted to give you a heads-up that I will be out of the office and unreachable next week. If possible, could we aim to finalize the job advertisement before I leave?

Once ChatGPT has provided the message text you need, you copy the text and paste it into a new message in your email client, address the message, insert the Subject line in the Subject box, and send the message on its way.

To have ChatGPT write a reply to a message, copy the message's text and paste it into the Send a Message box after a prompt such as this (and perhaps a line break you insert by pressing Shift+Enter):

(PROMPT) Read this message and write a polite reply saying no.

When ChatGPT has created the reply text, copy it. Click the Reply button in your email client to start the reply, paste in the text, and send the message.

Use ChatGPT to Check and Change the Tone of a Message or Document

ChatGPT can attempt to analyze the tone of a message or another document that you pass to it by pasting the text into the Send a Message box. I say "attempt to analyze" because, while ChatGPT is pretty good on formality and informality, warmth and coldness, verbosity and brevity, it's not fully comfortable with irony and sarcasm as of this writing. That leads to something of a problem: If you're not confident of your interpretation of a passage because you suspect it doesn't mean what it purports to say, you probably shouldn't rely on ChatGPT, because it likely won't know either — but may well deliver its interpretation with total confidence nonetheless.

To ask ChatGPT to check the tone of a passage, give a prompt such as this:

(PROMPT) Please analyze the tone of the following sentence:

> **No way, dude! That's totally rad! I'm bustin' a gut to get there.**

ChatGPT broke the sentence down in detail:

> *The tone of the sentence "No way, dude! That's totally rad! I'm bustin' a gut to get there." is informal, enthusiastic, and excited. The language used is casual and colloquial, often associated with*

informal conversation among friends. Phrases like "No way, dude" and "That's totally rad" suggest a strong positive reaction or surprise. "I'm bustin' a gut to get there" implies eagerness and anticipation, reinforcing the excited tone. Overall, the speaker seems to be expressing genuine enthusiasm and a sense of urgency.

To ask ChatGPT to rewrite a passage using a different tone, give a prompt such as this:

 Please rewrite the following sentence in formal language:

No way, dude! That's totally rad! I'm bustin' a gut to get there.

 Certainly, here's a more formal rendition of that sentence:

"I find that astonishing! It's truly remarkable! I'm making every effort to arrive promptly."

Ask for whatever tone you want — for example, a friendly tone, an assertive tone, or a diplomatic tone.

Use ChatGPT to Translate Communications

ChatGPT can translate text to and from an impressive selection of languages. Simply give a prompt that tells ChatGPT what you need. For example, if you receive an email in a foreign language, you could prompt ChatGPT as follows and then paste in the message:

 Translate the following text to English for me.

Or perhaps:

 Translate the following text to English and tell me what language it's in.

ChatGPT returns a translation. (And the source language, if you asked for it.)

Similarly, you could ask ChatGPT to translate a message you'd written into another language:

(PROMPT) **Translate the following message into German.**

Beware the Pitfalls of Machine Translation

ChatGPT and other machine translation services, such as Google Translate, deliver impressive results but may sometimes misinterpret complex phrasing or provide clunky text. When you're using these services to translate from a foreign language to English, such infelicities will likely be noticeable but harmless. But you should be somewhat wary when using machine translation to translate text to a foreign language that you do not understand, because such problems will be hard, if not impossible, for you to spot. Translating the translated text back to English may help you verify that the text has retained its meaning.

Use ChatGPT to Practice Conversations

You can use ChatGPT to practice conversations, albeit in a written format. Chapter 2 gives you examples of how to get ChatGPT to act as one interviewer at first and then as multiple interviewers.

As you'd imagine, you can use ChatGPT to practice other conversations that will benefit from preparation, such as asking your boss for a raise or (separately, I hope) explaining how a project went horribly wrong on your watch.

You can also use an "act-as" prompt to get ChatGPT to converse as someone who has a different native language and some difficulties with English. This approach might help you avoid linguistic trip wires and convey complex information clearly whether you're talking to native speakers or nonnative speakers (or both).

Here's an example of a prompt you might use:

 I'd like you to act as a Spanish speaker who has moderate but limited English. I want you to hold a conversation with me. I will say start by saying something in English. You will respond in English and wait for me to say something else. Do you understand?

Believe me, I felt pedantic writing that! But ChatGPT got the idea:

 Yes, I understand. Please start the conversation and I'll respond in my role as a Spanish speaker with moderate but limited English skills.

We then had a conversation, with ChatGPT fracturing its English. Here's an example:

 Oh, sorry for bad news. My good news is small. My plant in house, it grows new leaf. I very happy for this. And you, something good happen for you today?

Streamline Knowledge Sharing

Vital knowledge can easily get stuck in different silos within a company, sometimes jealously guarded by possessive gatekeepers but more often simply not shared because there's no easy way to share it. So any tool that can make it easier — or, better, effortless — to share knowledge across departments can be highly valuable.

In this section, we'll look at four ways in which you can use ChatGPT to streamline the sharing of information in your company: generating documents for sharing knowledge, creating training materials, summarizing information, and brainstorming to generate and develop ideas.

Using ChatGPT as a Knowledge Base

If your company programmatically integrates ChatGPT into a collaborative platform, such as a database or a customer relationship management (CRM) tool that contains your company's data, you may be able to use ChatGPT as a kind of knowledge base. In this scenario, you and your colleagues would be able to ask ChatGPT to return data from the company's own sources, making ChatGPT a convenient way to share information throughout the company.

Without this programmatic connection, which requires skilled programmers as of this writing, ChatGPT cannot access your company's data and so cannot answer questions about it.

Generate Documents for Sharing Knowledge

Historians tell us sharing knowledge via documents started in Mesopotamia more than 5,000 years ago. The method has moved on from cuneiform on clay tablets to digital files on networks and the web, but the principle remains the same: Someone writes down the information, and others can then read it and benefit (or sometimes suffer) from it.

These days, you can be that someone, preferably leveraging ChatGPT's help to quickly create documents from which your colleagues can benefit. Below are examples of prompts you might use to create widely useful types of documents such as reports, manuals, and presentations.

When you need a report, tell ChatGPT the topic, and provide any information that ChatGPT will need by pasting it into the Send a Message box. Here's an example:

Hi ChatGPT! Would you help me to write a report about the impact of e-bikes on the courier industry? Below, I'm pasting in data from a survey we performed that showed couriers on e-bikes were 15% faster and managed 23% more deliveries than couriers on regular bikes.

When you need to create a manual, keep in mind ChatGPT's maximum document length of 4096 tokens, where a single token can represent anything from a single character to an entire word. OpenAI suggests 15–20 pages of text as a rough guide of what 4096 tokens might cover. If your manual will need to be anywhere near this length, let alone longer, break up the manual into sections and create them separately.

Here's an example of creating an outline for a manual for an in-house software app:

I need to create a manual for our new in-house app. Please draw me up an outline with four parts: Getting the App, Navigating the Interface, Becoming Proficient, and Taking It to the Next Level.

Certainly, here's a draft structure for the manual of your new in-house app:

Part 1: Getting the App

1. Introduction:

- *Brief introduction of the app and its features.*
- *Who the app is intended for and what tasks it can help with.*

2. System Requirements:

- *Detail the necessary hardware and software requirements for the app.*
  . . .

Part 2: Navigating the Interface

1. Overview of the Interface:

- *Description of the main interface, buttons, icons, and where to find key features and settings.*
  . . .

You and ChatGPT can then work on the individual sections, keeping the file size of each section comfortably below the 4096-token limit.

If you need a presentation, ask ChatGPT for help with the outline and text for the slides. Creating the presentation file; choosing the presentation template and theme; and adding, graphics, audio, and video are up to you.

> **PROMPT** **Draw me up an outline for a presentation on Genetic Modification in Pets: Aligning Customer Requests with Ethical Guidelines. Nine slides, including an Introduction slide and a Questions slide at the end.**

NOTE The prompts in this section only scratch the surface of the many types of documents that ChatGPT can create for you or help you create. Other chapters in the book cover other types of documents:

- Chapter 3 shows you how to use ChatGPT to create various documents, including meeting agendas and meeting notes.
- Chapter 4 takes you through creating documents such as proposals and business letters.

Create Training Materials

Training is another highly effective way to share information with your colleagues, especially if you use role-play in scenarios that may occur during work — for example, upselling a customer during a sales call or dealing with a rapidly unfolding threat to the company.

You can get ChatGPT to create training scenarios for you. See Chapter 10 for information on creating such scenarios.

Summarize Information

Sometimes the problem you face when attempting to find the information you need on a topic is sorting the wheat from the chaff — locating the worthwhile grains of data in a field of low-quality material. If you're in this situation, use ChatGPT's Summarize command to have ChatGPT reduce articles or web pages to summaries that enable you to decide which are worth reading in full. See Chapter 5 for examples of how to use the Summarize command.

Brainstorm Ideas and Solutions

When you need to generate ideas for a specific purpose, set aside some time to work on it with ChatGPT. ChatGPT can be a terrific help for brainstorming, because you can make it play different roles, such as forcing you to think "outside the box" and approach a topic in different ways.

> **NOTE**   Perhaps the best thing about ChatGPT for brainstorming is its boundless patience when you want to really dig into a topic. You can keep prompting ChatGPT to think about things again, to generate other ideas, or to provide further examples for as long as you like — far beyond the point at which a human colleague would have decorated you with the dregs of their coffee and left the building.

To brainstorm using ChatGPT, you'll likely want to take the following steps. For clarity, I'll present a single extended example rather than several separate examples.

1. Establish the Topic on Which You're Brainstorming   Start by telling ChatGPT the topic you're brainstorming about. Here are three examples:

Hi ChatGPT! I want you to brainstorm with me. The topic is: How can we increase sales per customer?

ChatGPT responded with enthusiasm and offered suggestions immediately:

 Absolutely, I'd be happy to brainstorm with you. Here are several strategies that could help increase sales per customer:

1. ***Upselling and Cross-Selling****: Encourage customers to buy a more expensive version of the product they are considering (upselling) or to buy a related product (cross-selling). This could be done by showing comparisons and reviews highlighting the benefits of the premium product, or by suggesting relevant add-ons at the checkout.*

2. ***Loyalty Programs****: Implement a rewards program that encourages repeat purchases. Reward points could be accumulated with every purchase and redeemed for discounts, exclusive products, or other benefits. . . .*

ChatGPT provided these 10 suggestions at first:

- Upselling and Cross-Selling
- Loyalty Programs
- Bundling
- Personalized Recommendations
- Exclusive Products or Services
- Flexible Payment Options
- Improved Customer Service
- After-Sale Services
- Educate the Customers
- Flash Sales or Limited Time Offers

2. Ask ChatGPT for Further Ideas If Necessary

ChatGPT's initial suggestions may be enough for you to skip this step. But if not, prompt ChatGPT for further ideas to make sure you've got plenty to think about.

PROMPT That list is a good start. Can you give me 10 more ideas?

ChatGPT could, and did:

Certainly, here are ten more ideas to increase sales per customer:

1. **Subscription Services**: *Depending on your business, you might consider creating a subscription model where customers pay a monthly or annual fee for ongoing access to your products or services. This can drive a consistent, reliable revenue stream and increase overall customer spend.*

2. **Referral Programs**: *Implement a referral program that rewards customers for bringing new customers to your business. This not only can increase your customer base, but also incentivize current customers to buy more to make use of their rewards.*

   . . .

The second list of 10 suggestions looked like this:

- Subscription Services
- Referral Programs
- Product Customizations
- Experiential Retail
- Seasonal or Themed Promotions
- Product Upgrades
- Gamified Shopping
- Extended Warranties or Service Plans
- Value Packs
- Live Demonstrations or Webinars

3. Work with ChatGPT's Suggestions

Once ChatGPT has given you some suggestions that look promising, work with ChatGPT on them. For example, to follow up on ChatGPT's suggestion of Experiential Retail, you might prompt like this:

PROMPT **Please give me three or four examples of experiential retail.**

ChatGPT told me about Apple Stores, Nike Stores, Lush Cosmetics, and IKEA, which have "transformed shopping from a chore into an experience."

I got the idea, even though my idea of shopping involves as quick an exit as possible. (After paying, yes.) Next, I prompted ChatGPT:

PROMPT **Okay, explain gamified shopping to me.**

ChatGPT explained that this involves incorporating gaming elements to make shopping more engaging and rewarding — making it a first-person shopper game, if you will. Brands set challenges for customers to complete in order to win rewards or move up to the next level in a loyalty scheme.

4. Make ChatGPT Generate Questions

To explore an idea from different angles, you can tell ChatGPT to generate questions about it. For example, ChatGPT's initial suggestions included implementing a loyalty program to drive sales. You might prompt ChatGPT like this:

PROMPT **Tell me five questions we should consider before implementing a loyalty program.**

ChatGPT returned five questions, including "What are your goals?", "What type of loyalty program best fits your business model and customers?", and "How will you promote and manage the program?"

You might also challenge the idea more directly — for example:

 What are the disadvantages of implementing a loyalty program?

5. Have ChatGPT Summarize Ideas from the Brainstorming Session
When you finish the brainstorming session, ask ChatGPT to summarize the ideas you've discussed. Here's an example:

(PROMPT) Please summarize the ideas we just brainstormed. 500 words max.

7

ChatGPT Prompts for Web Development

IF YOUR DUTIES include creating web copy, web pages, or even entire websites, ChatGPT can be a valuable assistant. You can get ChatGPT to take on a wide range of duties—anything from analyzing competitive websites all the way through drafting web-page content to creating HTML, CSS, and scripts for you. This chapter points you toward the actions you're likely to find most immediately helpful.

For any of the prompts in this chapter that require full access to the web, such as analyzing a website, you'll need to use ChatGPT's Web Browsing Model. For other prompts, you may be able to use either the Web Browsing Model or another model. For example, you can have ChatGPT analyze a web page by pasting its contents into the Send a Message field instead of accessing the web page directly on its website.

Analyze Competitive Websites

If you're looking to improve your website, you'll likely want to know what your competitors' websites have to offer. A quick way to find out is to get ChatGPT to analyze them. Here are three prompts you might use, including the website's URL where the *URL* placeholder appears:

Analyze the following website and give me an overview of its content: *URL*

Analyze the following website from a design point of view. Tell me what the website does well and what it does more poorly. *URL*

 Analyze the website at *URL* for usability and create a 200-word report explaining it to me.

Summarize a Web Page

In Chapter 4, you saw how to use the "summarize" command to tell ChatGPT to give you the gist of a written document. You can do this with a web page as well. For example, with the Web Browsing Model enabled, you can give a prompt such as this:

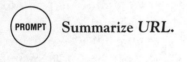 Summarize *URL*.

Or:

Summarize in 100 words *URL*.

Without the Web Browsing Model enabled, you need to copy the web page's content and paste it into ChatGPT. As usual, you're bound by ChatGPT's 4096-token limit for text input, so summarizing long pages may be problematic.

Analyze a Web Page for Keywords

With the Web Browsing Model enabled, you can ask ChatGPT to analyze a web page for keywords. For example:

(PROMPT) **Please analyze this web page and tell me the keywords: URL**

ChatGPT returned a list of "key terms and phrases that stand out." Without the Web Browsing Model enabled, you can copy the web page and paste it into ChatGPT with a prompt such as this:

(PROMPT) **Analyze the following text and tell me the 10 top keywords:**

You would then optionally press Shift+Enter to create a line break and mandatorily press Ctrl+V to paste in the text. As above, ChatGPT can accept text input of up to 4096 tokens, which may truncate longer web pages.

Identify What Your Website Needs

ChatGPT can help you to identify what your website needs. For example, if you're starting out with your website, you might start by prompting ChatGPT to create a sitemap for you:

Propose a sitemap for a static website that has a focus on cooking with onions.

Certainly! Here's a proposed sitemap for a static website focused on cooking with onions:

1. Home
   - *Introduction to the website and its purpose*
   - *Featured recipes or articles related to cooking with onions*

. . .

10. Contact

- Contact information for the website or its creators
- Feedback form or email address for inquiries or suggestions
- Links to social media profiles for further engagement

The sitemap looked good, but the contact form risks exposing contact details to a scraping attack, where online malefactors collect contact information for spamming or phishing. So:

 How can I implement a contact form on a static website in a way that is not highly susceptible to scraping-based spam attacks?

ChatGPT suggested six strategies for mitigating the risk of scraping-based spam attacks, ranging from using a CAPTCHA (for example, "click each square containing a car") to adding a hidden "honeypot field" that bots will fill in but people won't.

 Can I use an embedded element from a service that specializes in such fields?

ChatGPT said "yes" and suggested several form service providers that have spam-protection features, including Google reCAPTCHA and Formspree.

Create Web Pages

Once you've identified the web pages you need to create, have ChatGPT help you to create them. Start by giving ChatGPT a prompt that explains exactly what you want. Here's an example:

 Create a 500-word web page that explains the purpose of onions and their importance in cooking and in the human diet. Encode the web page in HTML.

Even though the prompt specifies a web page, you need to tell ChatGPT to encode it in HTML. Otherwise, ChatGPT gives you the text content for the web page, leaving you to handle the encoding.

Creating Web Pages with ChatGPT's Help

ChatGPT is more than capable of creating complete web pages. This capability is sometimes useful, such as when you're creating a sample website.

Normally, though, you'll want to use ChatGPT only to create the foundation or framework of a web page, and then write the rest of the content yourself (or have your colleagues write it). That way, you end up with an original web page that gives exactly the message you want and gives an authentic human feeling rather than the somewhat mechanical feeling that ChatGPT sometimes gives.

You might prefer to have the text content so that you can rewrite and enhance the page in a word processor rather than working in an HTML editor. If so, when the text is ready, you can prompt ChatGPT to convert it to HTML for you with a prompt such as this:

(PROMPT) **Convert the following text to an HTML web page:**

As usual, paste in the text, optionally preceding it with a line break (press Shift+Enter).

You might prompt ChatGPT to create a template for a particular type of web page, such as a blog post. Here's an example:

(PROMPT) **Can you write the HTML structure for a blog post page?**

ChatGPT created a straightforward HTML page for a blog post, including navigation links and a footer. ChatGPT made the main part of the post into an HTML article element.

What to Include in Your Prompt for Creating a Web Page

When prompting ChatGPT to create a web page for you, you'll need to specify at least the subject for the page. In most cases, specifying the approximate number of words is helpful, too, but sometimes you may want to let ChatGPT determine the initial length and then adjust it if necessary.

If you want the web page aimed at a particular target audience, tell ChatGPT what it is; otherwise, ChatGPT will write for a general audience. You might want to let ChatGPT write for the general audience first and see how closely the result fits your needs. If the text is close, you could improve it manually yourself; if the text needs rewriting, you could tell ChatGPT to rewrite it for the target audience before honing it further yourself.

If the web page is to explain a particular problem and position your company's product as a solution to it, give ChatGPT the details. Likewise, if the web page is to end with a clear call to action to tell the reader what you expect them to do, instruct ChatGPT to insert that call to action.

Review and Improve a Web Page's Content

Whether you've created a web page from scratch or enlisted Chat-GPT's help in creating it, you can ask ChatGPT to suggest ways to improve the page—and then make those improvements. Here are a couple of examples:

 Review the following web page content for grammatical errors and clarity of language. Suggest keyword optimizations I might make.

As usual, you'd paste in the web page content, optionally pressing Shift+Enter to create a new line first.

For the example web page, ChatGPT responded:

Sure, let's review this for grammar, clarity, and keyword optimization.

The content is generally clear and engaging, with a good mix of storytelling and informational writing. The tone is casual and friendly, which is likely to resonate with many readers.

However, there are a few areas where the language could be clarified or simplified for better readability. Additionally, I've identified some potential keyword optimizations . . .

The specific suggestions followed. Most were on target and helpful.

 Suggest ways of improving this home page for a blog site.

The provided home page for the sample blog site is a good starting point, but it can be improved in several ways. Here are some suggestions:

1. Add a favicon: Include a favicon.ico file in the root directory of your website. This small icon will appear in the browser's tab, improving the visual identity of your site.

Many of ChatGPT's 10 suggestions sounded good. So:

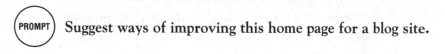 **Please implement a favicon link, an appealing CSS header, a navigation menu, some semantic HTML elements, a visually distinct footer, and a better means of linking the CSS file. Also, add meta tags.**

Certainly! Here's an updated version of the home page with the requested improvements: . . .

Create an External CSS File

You can have ChatGPT create CSS files for you. For example, you might point ChatGPT at a web page and give a prompt like this:

 Write me an external CSS file derived from this web page.

As usual, you'd supply the URL if you're using the Web Browsing Model. If not, you'd paste in the text of the web page.

If you have HTML pages that use inline styles, you can have ChatGPT transition those styles to an internal style sheet to make the page easier to maintain and update. Here's an example:

 In the following HTML file, change each instance of an inline style to a style using an internal style sheet.

 To replace the inline styles with an internal style sheet, you need to add a <style> block in the <head> section of the HTML document and create appropriate CSS selectors. We'll create two classes: .table1 and .table2, which will be assigned to your tables respectively. Here is the updated HTML:

As you can see, ChatGPT handled that task nicely. Likewise, ChatGPT did a neat job of switching an HTML document from internal styles to an external CSS file that it created. Here's the prompt that I used:

 In the following HTML file, please change each instance of an internal style to a style in an external CSS file. Create the CSS file and name it styles42.css.

Write Scripts for Web Pages

As well as being adept in creating and manipulating HTML and CSS, ChatGPT can handle a wide range of programming languages. We'll look at this capability in more detail in Chapter 8, but while we're talking about web work, you might want to have ChatGPT write scripts for your website.

All you need is a suitable prompt. Here's an example:

 Write a Python script that generates a summary page with the title and first few lines of each file in /blog-posts/*. html, linking to them much like how WordPress summarizes posts in reverse chronological order.

 Certainly! Here's an example Python script that generates a summary page with the title and first few lines of each HTML file in the /blog-posts/ directory, linking to them in reverse chronological order:

This script required having the BeautifulSoup library installed, but ChatGPT was happy to change to a different library when I prompted it:

 Could you modify the script to use LXML instead?

 Certainly! Here's the modified version of the script that uses lxml instead of BeautifulSoup for parsing the HTML files:

This version of the script worked fine, but it took a while to run. But a quick prompt was all it took to persuade ChatGPT to rewrite the script in Rust, which ran much faster:

 Please write a similar implementation using Rust.

ChatGPT Prompts for Programming

ALONG WITH THE skills you've read about in other chapters, ChatGPT is pretty good at programming. That might seem strange; but ChatGPT is a large language model, and programs are written in various programming languages, most of which obey far more formal structures than English and the other human languages that ChatGPT handles so well.

If you're a programmer or you work in software development, try integrating ChatGPT into your workflow and see what it can do for you. Even if your interest in programming is casual and you just need to hack together a quick-and-dirty Word VBA macro or a Python script to perform a one-time task, ChatGPT may be able to save you time and effort.

Let's start with the $64 million question . . .

Which Programming Languages Can ChatGPT Help You With?

The short answer is: most of them. Python, Java, JavaScript, C, C++, C#, Ruby, PHP, Swift, Go, R, SQL, TypeScript, VBA, Rust, and MATLAB—ChatGPT is happy to help you with all of these, and more.

Beyond these programming languages, ChatGPT can help with shell scripting using tools such as Bash and PowerShell. It can also assist you with HTML and CSS, which aren't really programming languages but are universally used for websites. (Look back to Chapter 7 for more on HTML and CSS.)

As of this writing, ChatGPT's training data runs up to September 2021, so ChatGPT is best informed about programming languages that were current then and before. If you're working with newer programming languages, such as Carbon (aka Carbon-Lang, introduced in 2022) or A Tensor Language (ATL, also new in 2022), ChatGPT will have less information but can search on the Web if you're using the Web Browsing Model.

How Can ChatGPT Help You with Programming?

ChatGPT can help with programming in five main ways:

- **Conceptualize the program or the code goal.** Before you begin typing code, you'll normally want to describe the program or the other code object you plan to create. If the program is complex, consider breaking it down into components. ChatGPT can help you to define what the code should do.
- **Write the code.** Once you've clearly delineated your coding goal, it's time to start writing—or time to have ChatGPT start writing for you. ChatGPT can not only help you map out the structure of the program or object, but it can also write complete code for you.
- **Debug the code.** Sometimes, ChatGPT's—or your—initial version of the code won't work. When this happens, you can ask ChatGPT to debug it for you.
- **Refactor the code.** Once the code is working, you can get ChatGPT to restructure the code to reduce its complexity and make it easier to read and maintain.
- **Optimize the code.** When the code is structured the way you want, you can tell ChatGPT to optimize the code to make it run faster, consume fewer resources, or both.

We'll look at each of these five steps with examples in the following sections.

Conceptualize the Program or Code Goal

Your first step is usually to conceptualize the program or the code that you want to create. Here are examples of prompts you might use to enlist ChatGPT's help:

 Which programming language would I use to analyze large quantities of data?

ChatGPT suggested languages such as Python, R, SQL, and Julia, explaining the pros and cons of each.

 Write a plan for creating a Python script to prompt the user to enter information that the script then stores in an Excel worksheet.

ChatGPT provided a detailed plan, from setting up the Python environment and creating a new script all the way through to testing the script and expanding it to handle more complex scenarios.

 Using the Go language, I want to create a function that adds two floating-point numbers and converts the result to an integer. Can you tell me how to get started?

Again, ChatGPT provided full details, including a warning that Go uses static typing, which means you need to specify the data types of the inputs and outputs the function uses.

Write Code

To get ChatGPT to write code, tell it which language to use and what code to create. Here are three examples:

 Write a "Hello, Universe!" program in C, including comments explaining each statement.

ChatGPT returned a program with comments explaining what it does. You can click the Copy Code button to copy the code, paste it into your C compiler, and run it.

 Implement a bubble sort algorithm in Rust that prints out every operation it performs so I can understand how the result is achieved.

ChatGPT returned a "simple implementation of the Bubble Sort algorithm in Rust" with an example that you can copy and a detailed explanation.

 How can I use the Python ruamel.yaml library to get two dictionaries: one for key-value pairs of tag and text, and one for key-value pairs of tag and comment for tag lines that include comments?

ChatGPT recommended using the CommentedMap object in the ruamel.yaml parser and provided an example with a detailed explanation.

NOTE   You can also ask ChatGPT for help with specific programming structures. For example, you might ask:

(PROMPT) **What kinds of loop expressions can I use in Rust?**

Or:

(PROMPT) **Show me how a while loop works in Rust.**

Debug Code

When you have code that isn't working, see if ChatGPT can help you debug it. ChatGPT is good with code that doesn't run at all, code that partly runs but produces specific errors, and code that runs apparently successfully but produces the wrong output because of logical errors.

Debug Code That Won't Run

If ChatGPT has created or worked with the code in this chat, you can simply refer ChatGPT to the code. If ChatGPT doesn't know the code, you'll need to paste it in. Give a prompt such as this:

 The following code doesn't run. Please review it and tell me what is wrong.

Press Shift+Enter to create a new line, and then paste in the code by pressing Ctrl+V.

> **NOTE**   You can specify the programming language the code uses if you want, but you don't usually need to, as ChatGPT works out which language it is.

If ChatGPT can identify the problem, it returns a brief explanation of what the problem is and why it occurs. It also returns a version of the code, updated with the fix it has identified, for you to try.

To give the code a good trial, you may want to ask ChatGPT for test cases. Here's an example prompt:

(PROMPT) **Give me four test cases for testing the code you just fixed.**

ChatGPT instantly returned those test cases, explaining what each does (such as "Test with a null string") and showing the output each should produce.

Debug Code That Produces Specific Errors

If your code produces a specific error, such as a SyntaxError error in Python, give ChatGPT the code and ask why that error occurred. Here's an example:

(PROMPT) **Why does this Python statement throw a SyntaxError?**

Press Shift+Enter to create a new line, and then paste in the offending statement by pressing Ctrl+V.

ChatGPT returned an explanation, such as the following, and the corrected code.

*The syntax error is occurring because you're missing parentheses around the string you're trying to print. In Python 3, the **print** statement was replaced with a **print()** function.*

Debug Code That Produces Logical Errors

Sometimes your code will run without throwing an error, but it will give a result that you can tell is wrong. This is usually the result of a *logical* error, which is an error that has to do with the logic of what the code does rather than the syntax of the code.

When your code produces a logical error, you can ask ChatGPT what's wrong. For example:

(PROMPT) **Why does the following code return a positive number instead of a negative number?**

ChatGPT analyzed the code, provided a detail explanation, and gave me a fixed version of the code to try.

Refactor Code

By this point, your code should be working. Unless you were hacking together a quick fix to solve a problem that will never arise again, it's not yet time to find laurels to rest on. Instead, you should probably refactor your code, reducing its complexity and making it easier to read and maintain. Better yet, have ChatGPT refactor the code for you.

> **NOTE** Refactoring code and optimizing code overlap to some extent, but you would normally refactor code before optimizing it. Apart from making code easier to read and to maintain, refactoring may also identify areas for optimizing the code.

Here are four examples of prompts for refactoring code:

 Please refactor this code to make it easy to read and easy to maintain.

 I want to make this code more maintainable. Can you find an existing library that extracts data as I'm doing here?

 In the following code, please replace the if-then-else chain with a case statement.

 Refactor this code, moving discrete functionality into a set of functions to reduce nesting.

For each of these examples, you would provide ChatGPT with the code unless ChatGPT already has access to the code in the active chat.

Optimize Code

Once you've refactored the code to your preferred end, you can have ChatGPT optimize the code.

Here are two examples of prompts you might use to ask ChatGPT to optimize your code. As usual, you would paste in the code unless ChatGPT already has access to it in this chat.

Identify any likely performance issues in the C# code below and tell me how to fix them.

 I'd like you to help me identify the most computationally-expensive operations in this code and tell me how to make it run faster.

You might also ask for optimization advice in general terms without giving ChatGPT your code. Here's an example:

I'm using Python with LXML and trying to get all elements with a "persist" attribute. My code iterates over every element and checks it for the "persist" attribute. The code runs slowly. Is there a better way to do this?

ChatGPT recommended using the XPath language to directly select XML elements that have the "persist" attribute.

9

ChatGPT Prompts for HR and Training

IN THIS CHAPTER, we'll look at ChatGPT prompts you can deploy for HR and training in your company or organization. (For simplicity's sake, we'll assume it's a company from here on.) We'll start by looking at how to get ChatGPT to draft job descriptions and job ads for you, and then move along to creating onboarding materials and developing scenarios for role-play training. Finally, we'll cover enlisting ChatGPT's assistance to solicit feedback from your company's employees.

> ### Understanding ChatGPT's Input and Output Limitations
>
> In this chapter, we'll bump up against ChatGPT's limitations. As of this writing, the key limitations are that ChatGPT can receive input only through the Send a Message box or by using the Web Browsing Model and accessing public websites; and that it can output data only as text in the browser window or in the ChatGPT app.
>
> *(continued)*

That means you can't, for example, hook up ChatGPT to your company's database to read existing data or to input new data; nor can you point it to sources of information on your company's internal network. The only way around these limitations is by performing some heavy-duty programming, which I'm assuming you won't be doing.

Despite these limitations, you can still gain great benefits from using ChatGPT, but you will need to perform all file-related operations yourself rather than have ChatGPT perform them for you.

Draft Job Descriptions and Job Ads

ChatGPT can help you write job descriptions and job ads. This can be a terrific time-saver, especially if you don't have previous job descriptions or job ads to use as examples.

How Do Job Descriptions and Job Ads Differ?

A *job description* spells out the responsibilities, duties, and requirements of a job in detail. A company typically uses job descriptions internally to make clear what each job involves and to provide evaluation points during performance reviews. A job description would typically have sections such as Job Title, Company Overview, Job Description, Responsibilities, Qualifications, Compensation, and What We Offer.

A *job ad* is a shorter document created to attract applicants for the job. A company typically makes job ads public on websites or physical job boards to attract potential applicants.

Draft Job Descriptions

Let's start with the job descriptions. Here are three examples of prompts asking ChatGPT to draft assorted job descriptions:

 Hi ChatGPT! Help me draft a job description for a Risk Analyst position with our financial services firm. The applicant will need a degree in accounting and five years' experience.

ChatGPT produced a detailed job description that began like this:

 Job Title: Risk Analyst

Company Overview: [Company Name] is a dynamic, progressive financial services firm that prides itself on being at the forefront of innovation and excellence in the finance industry. Our commitment to our clients is matched only by our dedication to our employees' professional growth and development. As we continue to expand, we're now seeking a talented, detail-oriented Risk Analyst to join our team.

Job Description:

The Risk Analyst at [Company Name] will be responsible for evaluating and forecasting potential risks while providing strategic advice to our leadership team. This role requires an analytical mindset, excellent problem-solving skills, and an ability to work under pressure.

 Write me a job description for a Sales Manager at our recreational clothing company. The candidate will need to be hard-charging but sensitive to the varying needs of our diverse customer base. Pay is commensurate with experience, plus a fast-ramping commission scheme.

ChatGPT included the terms "hard-charging" and "fast-ramping" in the job description, which also included this detailed list of responsibilities:

 Responsibilities:

- *Develop and implement strategic sales plans aligned with the company's goals to drive sales growth.*
- *Lead, coach, and mentor a team of sales representatives to improve performance and reach sales targets.*
- *Understand the needs of our diverse customer base and adjust sales strategies accordingly.*
- *Build and maintain strong relationships with key customers, stakeholders, and industry professionals.*
- *Analyze sales metrics to forecast sales growth and identify opportunities for improvement.*
- *Work closely with the marketing department to ensure consistent messaging and alignment with sales strategies.*
- *Monitor competitors, market conditions, and product developments.*

PROMPT **Okay, we need to hire a Collection Specialist for our Delinquency Rehabilitation Team. Qualifications: Business degree; 3+ years' collection experience; strong analytical skills; excellent telephone, written, and spoken communication skills; proven ability to exceed collection targets in previous roles. Motivated self-starter with outsize work ethic able to perform with light supervision. Give me a job description with all that, stat.**

Here, too, ChatGPT did a bang-up job. Here's the Qualifications section of the job description:

Qualifications:

- A Bachelor's degree in Business, Finance, or a related field.
- Minimum of three years' experience in collections or a related role.
- Exceptional telephone, written, and verbal communication skills.
- Strong analytical skills with the ability to make informed decisions.
- Proven track record of exceeding collection targets.
- Self-motivated, with the ability to work independently and minimal supervision.
- Demonstrated high-level work ethic and integrity.

Draft Job Ads

Now, let's move on to the job ads. Often, these will be related to the job descriptions, so if you've just had ChatGPT write the job description in the same chat, you may want to have ChatGPT work from that.

For example, you could ask ChatGPT to write a job ad for the Collection Specialist like this:

 Please write a job advertisement for the Collection Specialist job for which you just created the job description.

ChatGPT returned a job advertisement that started like this:

 Job Advertisement:

Collection Specialist Wanted! Join Our Delinquency Rehabilitation Team!

Are you a seasoned Collection Specialist with a knack for exceeding targets? Do you pride yourself on your exceptional communication skills and your ability to solve complex problems? If so, [Company Name] may have the perfect opportunity for you.

If you haven't had ChatGPT write the job description, paste it in after the prompt, optionally entering a line break (press Shift+Enter) between the two:

I'd like you to create a job ad for a Content Management Specialist for our Tech Support Team. Here's the job description:

If you don't have a job description, no problem — just have ChatGPT write the job ad, and then prompt for any changes needed. Here's an example of a job ad with a maximum length:

Put together a job ad for an experienced Accountant to provide maternity cover for three months. We're an e-commerce startup, but people are friendly and the office is an oasis of calm and good sense. The job ad needs to be 100 words maximum.

Job Ad:

Temp Accountant Needed at E-commerce Startup!

[Company Name] is seeking an experienced Accountant for a three-month maternity cover. Join our friendly team and enjoy our oasis of calm in a dynamic e-commerce setting. Responsibilities: all-round accounting duties, ensuring financial accuracy and compliance. Requirements: proven accounting experience, detail-oriented, solid analytical skills. Come, contribute your expertise in our exciting journey. Apply now!

I figured we needed to sell the job a little harder:

You know, let's not say that we're a startup. Mention our canteen — free meals prepared by a chef — and say we're five minutes' walk from public transit.

Job Ad:

Accountant Wanted for 3-Month Maternity Cover!

Join our friendly team at [Company Name]! Looking for an experienced Accountant to uphold our financial accuracy and compliance. Perks? Our canteen provides free meals by a personal chef, and we're just a five-minute walk from public transit. Apply now to contribute your expertise to our dynamic e-commerce team.

One more round of changes, and the job ad was good to post.

Can I Get ChatGPT to Read and Evaluate Resumes for Me?

Yes, you can. But don't get too excited yet. Because of ChatGPT's limitations on accessing external files, you need to copy each resume's text and paste it into the Send a Message box to give it to ChatGPT.

If the resumes are short, you can paste in several resumes at a time without running up against the 4096-token maximum length. If the resumes are longer, you'll need to paste in one at a time. It's usually easier to paste in one at a time so that the prompt doesn't have to explain to ChatGPT that the number of resumes will vary.

Here's an example of the type of prompt you might use to get ChatGPT to read the resumes. You'll want to customize it to your needs.

> **PROMPT**
>
> **Hi, ChatGPT! I want you to read 20 resumes for me. I'll give them to you one at a time, okay? In each resume, find the applicant's name and address, and store them. Also find whether the applicant has the Cisco Certified Network Associated certification, CCNA, and store that information, too. When you've finished reading one resume, ask me for the next resume. After reading**

(continued)

> **all 20 resumes, give me a table of the applicants' names, addresses, and CCNA certification (Yes or No). Ready for the first resume? I'll paste it into the Send a Message box.**
>
> When ChatGPT tells you it's ready, paste in the first resume and press Enter.

NOTE   You can also have ChatGPT write HR letters, such as employment offer letters and termination letters. See Chapter 4 for examples of prompts for writing business letters.

Develop Onboarding and Training Materials

When you've succeeded in hiring an employee, you'll want to onboard them smoothly so as to get them settled down satisfactorily in the company and contributing to the bottom line. Once they're settled, you'll likely want to encourage them to develop their skills and abilities through ongoing training.

ChatGPT can help you create many different types of onboarding and training materials. In this section, we'll look at three types of materials that give you an idea of the range of possibilities:

- A customized onboarding guide for a new employee
- A standard checklist of tasks each new employee should complete in their first few days or weeks
- Training scenarios for employees to role-play

Create an Onboarding Guide for a New Employee

ChatGPT can quickly draw up a customized onboarding guide for a new employee. The process isn't effortless on your part, because you need to give ChatGPT access to the information it needs, but the results are usually highly worthwhile.

Assemble the following information in a text format you can paste into ChatGPT's Send a Message box:

- **Company Information.** What you want the employee to know about the company's history, its goals for the future, its values, and its culture. This information can be general for all employees' onboarding guides.
- **Job Specifics.** The new employee's role and responsibilities. Include the department, the employee's immediate supervisor or manager, and details of their expected performance.
- **Training Requirements.** Include details of any training the new employee will have to complete, such as job-specific training or compliance training.
- **Key Policies and Procedures.** Include information about the company's policies and codes of conduct.
- **Tools and Resources.** List the tools and resources the employee will use, such as software, hardware, and online services.
- **Key Contacts.** List the people with whom you expect the new employee to interact frequently, such as team members in their department or point people in other departments.
- **Performance Goals.** List the goals you expect the employee to meet within a given time frame, such as their first three months. Detail any key performance indicators (KPIs) you will use for evaluation.
- **Initial Schedule.** Mark key dates — such as mandatory meetings, training sessions, and deadlines — on a customized calendar for the employee.
- **Benefits and Perks.** Provide information about the benefits package and perks the company provides.
- **FAQs.** Provide access to a Frequently Asked Questions list (preferably on the company's intranet).

Once you've lined up all this information, you can prompt ChatGPT to create an onboarding guide. Here's an example:

> **(PROMPT)** **Create an onboarding guide for Joanna Mathis, our new Marketing Assistant. I'm giving you all the information below to create the guide: company information, Joanna's job details and training requirements, and so on.**

Press Shift+Enter to insert a line break, and then paste in the information.

Create a Checklist of Tasks for New Employees

To help each new employee find their feet, you may want to provide them with a standard checklist of tasks to complete during their early days, such as meeting with key individuals, setting up email accounts and other credentials, and completing formal paperwork (be it real or virtual).

If you don't have such a checklist, ask ChatGPT for help in creating one. To get started, you might use a prompt such as this:

PROMPT **Write a checklist of tasks for our new employees to complete during their first week with us.**

ChatGPT returned a detailed five-day plan that started like this:

 Sure! Here is a suggested checklist for a new hire's first week:

Day 1: Orientation Day

Meet the team and introduction to key company personnel

Get an office tour (physical or virtual)

Set up workstation (hardware/software)

Review the company's mission and vision

Introduction to company's products/services

Review company culture and core values

Introduction to company policies (HR policies, IT policies, etc.)

Day 2: Role Clarification and Expectations

Overview of job role and responsibilities

Introduction to immediate supervisor or manager . . .

If ChatGPT's suggested checklist requires changes, just prompt it to make them. For example:

Please reschedule "Introduction to immediate supervisor or manager" from Day 2 to Day 1.

ChatGPT made this change instantly.

Create Training Scenarios

To enable your employees to develop their skills and gain confidence in new areas, you can have ChatGPT create training scenarios that deliver targeted role-play in a controlled context.

For example, say you need your IT department to practice responding to a computer virus infection. You might prompt ChatGPT like this:

Please generate a training scenario for our IT department to practice responding to a computer virus infection. The scenario begins with the IT department receiving a phone call from the Marketing Director, who reports angrily that the Marketing computers have stopped working one by one and demands that IT fix the problem.

ChatGPT produced a six-phase scenario that started like this:

Scenario: Operation Code Red — Combatting a Potential Virus Infection

Phase 1 — Detection & Reporting

The IT department receives an urgent and irate call from the Marketing Director, complaining about an unusual situation where Marketing's computers have been shutting down one after the other. She demands immediate attention and resolution to the problem.

Phase 2 — Initial Response & Assessment

The IT team's first responder takes the call, reassures the Marketing Director that the issue is being taken seriously, and immediately starts gathering information: . . .

Similarly, you might instruct ChatGPT to give the Sales department some grief:

> **(PROMPT) Write me a training scenario for the Sales department. Their most important client called to cancel all his repeating orders because the most recent invoice contained an arithmetic error in his disfavor.**

ChatGPT wrote a scenario titled "Handling a Key Client Crisis — Invoice Error Fallout" that put the Sales department through the wringer.

Gather Feedback

You probably know from hard-won experience that happy employees tend to be more productive than disgruntled employees. A good way to help keep employees happy is to listen to their concerns and suggestions by soliciting feedback from them. Feedback may not only enable you to head off problems before they fester, but may also bring to light bright ideas for improving communication, streamlining processes, or developing new products.

What's not to like? Well, you need to expend time and effort implementing a mechanism to gather the feedback. But ChatGPT can help you with that — though perhaps not quite as much as you'd like, at least as of this writing.

Understand What Kind of Feedback Mechanism ChatGPT Can Help You Implement

Here's an imaginary feedback mechanism: a version of ChatGPT customized to solicit feedback from employees, parse it, and direct it to the appropriate recipients. For example, when an employee fires up this feedback bot, it asks them how they're doing and what's on their mind; gets the details, asking sensible follow-up questions; enters the feedback in a database; summarizes the feedback; and sends the summary to the appropriate people, such as to HR and the employee's supervisor.

If that sounds like just the ticket to you — sorry, it's not in the cards as of this writing, although it might be doable before too long, as OpenAI increases ChatGPT's connectivity.

So what *can* you do? You can take various approaches, but a typical one might look something like this and use surveys for implementation:

1. **Decide what you want feedback on.** For example, you might survey employees about their job satisfaction or about the work environment. ChatGPT can offer suggestions of what types of feedback to solicit.

2. **Create survey questions.** ChatGPT can help you draft the questions.

3. **Implement the survey.** You'd use a survey platform, such as Google Forms or SurveyMonkey (www.surveymonkey.com), to distribute the survey, collect the employees' response, and tabulate the results. ChatGPT can't help directly with this, but it can cheer you on silently from the sidelines.

4. **Analyze the survey responses.** You'd paste the response data you wanted to analyze into ChatGPT and tell it what kind of analysis you wanted.

5. **Create a feedback report.** ChatGPT can help you write a report summarizing the feedback results, highlighting insights gained, and suggesting actions your company might take.

The following subsections take you through the above five steps.

Decide What You Want Feedback On

Your first step in setting up the feedback mechanism is to decide what subject you want feedback on. Let's say it's the work environment.

You could prompt ChatGPT to suggest different aspects of the work environment to survey:

PROMPT **I want to get feedback on this company's work environment. Please identify five aspects of the work environment.**

ChatGPT suggested these five aspects: Physical Environment, Company Culture, Communication, Work-Life Balance, and Recognition and Reward.

Fair enough. Let's go with Physical Environment.

Create Survey Questions

Once you've chosen the subject on which you want feedback, you can have ChatGPT help you create survey questions. You can use either open-ended questions or Likert-scale questions, which are written as statements but usually termed "questions" (see the nearby sidebar, "Should You Use Open-Ended Questions or Likert Scale Questions?"). For example, you might prompt ChatGPT like this for open-ended questions:

PROMPT **Write five open-ended survey questions about the physical environment of this company.**

ChatGPT returned five open-ended questions including these three, the third, fourth, and fifth questions in the list:

3. *How comfortable do you feel with the facilities (restrooms, kitchen, break areas, etc.) provided in the office? Please explain why.*

4. *If you were given the opportunity to change or improve one thing about the physical environment, what would it be and why?*

5. *Can you provide specific examples of how the company has responded to your needs or concerns about the physical work environment?*

Here's an example of a prompt for Likert-scale questions:

 Write five Likert-scale survey questions about the physical environment of this company.

ChatGPT returned five Likert-scale questions including these three:

1. *The physical workspace provided by the company is conducive to productivity.*
2. *The company ensures a clean and healthy working environment.*
3. *The office layout encourages collaboration and interaction among employees.*

Should You Use Open-Ended Questions or Likert-Scale Questions?

In your surveys, you can use either open-ended questions or questions that use the Likert scale. An open-ended question is one that the survey respondent can answer however they choose, such as "How could we improve the work environment?" A Likert-scale question is a statement to which the respondent chooses a value on a five-point scale: 1 (Strongly Disagree), 2 (Disagree), 3 (Undecided), 4 (Agree), or 5 (Strongly Agree).

The upside of open-ended questions is that respondents can answer with rich qualitative data. The downside is that such data is hard to quantify.

The upside of Likert-scale questions is that they deliver quantitative data that you (or ChatGPT) can analyze relatively easily. The downside is that the gradations of data are relatively coarse, and the single-value answer prevents the respondent from giving a nuanced answer. For example, if the question states "This company has a positive work environment," and the respondent strongly agrees but has one major gripe, how should they answer? Perhaps with 4 (Agree), because their true answer would be 5 (Strongly Agree), but they're deducting a point for the gripe they cannot express?

Implement the Survey

Once you've decided on your questions, you can load them into a new survey on your preferred survey platform and distribute the survey to the appropriate employees. There's not much ChatGPT can do to help you with this step unless you need help using the survey platform — in which case, simply ask ChatGPT.

The survey platform will typically process the responses and tabulate the results for you.

Analyze the Survey Responses

After retrieving the survey response data from the survey platform, you can paste the data you want to analyze into ChatGPT and prompt it to perform the kind of analysis you want, such as a descriptive analysis or a sentiment analysis. Look back to Chapter 5 for coverage of the various types of data analysis ChatGPT can and cannot perform.

Create a Feedback Report

When ChatGPT has analyzed the survey data to your satisfaction, ask it to help you write a report based on the data. Here is an example:

Hi ChatGPT! You know that data you just analyzed for me? I'd like you to draft a report summarizing the survey's findings and suggesting the three most important actions we could take to increase employee satisfaction with the company's physical environment.

10

ChatGPT Prompts for Sales and Marketing

IN THIS CHAPTER, we'll look at several ways in which you can use Chat-GPT to boost your company's Sales and Marketing departments. We'll start by examining how to have ChatGPT create marketing content, such as blog posts, press releases, and marketing emails. After that, we'll see how to get ChatGPT to create sales content, using product descriptions and sales presentations as our examples. Toward the end of the chapter, we'll cover how to use ChatGPT to engage with customers via email, either drafting individual messages or drafting batches of messages.

In addition to the topics covered in this chapter, you may want to look at the following three topics in other chapters:

- The section "Write Copy" in Chapter 4 shows you prompts for creating copy for ads, social media, and so on.
- The section "Analyze Data" in Chapter 5 shows you prompts for performing various types of analysis on data you have collected.
- The section "Create Training Scenarios" in Chapter 9 demonstrates prompting ChatGPT to write scenarios for training staff. For example, you might have ChatGPT create scenarios to train your sales staff to eliminate roadblocks and close deals.

Understanding the Two Means of Interacting with ChatGPT

When you are working interactively with ChatGPT, it can receive input in two ways: either by having you type or paste data into the Send a Message box or by using the Web Browsing Model and accessing public websites. ChatGPT cannot open files on your company's network or intranet to get data, and you cannot connect it to a database. For interactive work, ChatGPT has only one way to output data — by displaying it in the browser window or in the ChatGPT app.

The alternative to working interactively is to use OpenAI's Application Programming Interface (API) to access ChatGPT programmatically. API access enables you to pass data to ChatGPT from other apps, greatly increasing the range of actions you can make ChatGPT perform, such as generating leads and qualifying sales prospects.

The downside is that working with the API requires experienced programmers. This book assumes that you will be working with ChatGPT interactively and performing all file-related actions yourself rather than working through the API.

Create Marketing Content

If you're working in marketing, make the most of ChatGPT as an assistant. ChatGPT is eternally eager to shoulder more than its fair share of the burden and can help you create a wide range of materials, including blog posts, social media content, and press releases. It can draft various types of email messages, such as newsletters and product announcements. And if you lack a marketing plan, ChatGPT can draw one up for you. The following subsections show you prompts for creating these materials.

Write Blog Posts

If you have a blog, you can get ChatGPT to write posts for it by giving brief instructions on what you want. Here are two examples:

 Write a blog post about the advantages and disadvantages of mechanical keyboards. Conclude that mechanical keyboards are best for heavy-duty text entry.

ChatGPT wrote a nicely structured post titled "The Pros and Cons of Mechanical Keyboards: A Boon for Heavy-Duty Typing," ending with the conclusion I requested.

 Write a 200-word blog post discussing whether the use of calculators should be allowed in math tests.

ChatGPT concluded the blog post like this:

 However, it's crucial to strike a balance. Calculators should be introduced once students have a solid foundation in fundamental arithmetic skills, to ensure they complement learning rather than replace it. Ultimately, the discerning use of calculators in math tests could lead to a richer understanding of mathematical concepts and more efficient problem-solving strategies.

Create Other Social Media Content

ChatGPT is equally happy to create content for social media platforms other than blogs. This section shows three examples of prompts you might use.

NOTE   Given its text-based nature, ChatGPT is better suited for creating textual content for social media platforms such as Facebook, LinkedIn, Twitter, Threads, and Bluesky than for working on primarily visual platforms such as Instagram,

YouTube, TikTok, Pinterest, or Snapchat. However, you can use ChatGPT for purposes such as writing video descriptions on YouTube or creating pin descriptions on Pinterest. You might also use ChatGPT to brainstorm ideas for Snapchat Stories.

Let's start with a post for Facebook:

 Write a Facebook post announcing our new cooking workshop at noon on Saturday: Tex-Mex Classics! Everyone welcome to the livestream; if you'll attend in person, book a place and bring your appetite!

ChatGPT returned a post bursting with enthusiasm and emojis, which ended like this (emojis elided):

 Get ready for a sizzling Saturday full of Tex-Mex goodness. We can't wait to see you there, either online or in person!

Bon appétit, amigos!

#TexMexClassics   #CookingWorkshop   #FoodiesUnite #SpiceUpYourLife

With a quick change (from *Bon appétit* to *Buen provecho*), the post was good to go.

Next, a company update for LinkedIn:

 Write a company update for me to post on LinkedIn. Next week, we're launching Penultimate Protein Pro, our new smart nutrition solution. It's for serious athletes and weekend warriors alike. Stress how this rounds out our Performance line of products. Invite our followers to give us feedback on their favorite ways of consuming Penultimate Protein Pro.

ChatGPT created a lively company update that started thus:

Exciting News Alert!

Next week, we're thrilled to introduce our latest innovation —
Penultimate Protein Pro — the smart nutrition solution for both
serious athletes and weekend warriors. We've harnessed the
power of cutting-edge nutrition science to create a product that
truly champions performance and wellness.

Penultimate Protein Pro is more than just a protein supplement; it's
a game-changer that supports muscle recovery, energy replenish-
ment, and overall wellness. Whether you're pushing your limits
in the gym or conquering the weekend hike, our new solution will
ensure you're fueled and ready for whatever comes your way.

In a store near you now!
We need to plug Penultimate Protein Pro on Twitter, too:

Write a tweet announcing our launch of Penultimate Pro-
tein Pro next Wednesday. We're offering a 2-for-1
early-bird deal.

BIG NEWS! Next Wednesday, we're launching Penultimate Pro-
tein Pro — the game-changer your fitness routine has been wait-
ing for! Be an early bird and snag our exclusive 2-for-1 deal at
launch. Fuel your performance, double the value! #Penulti-
mateProteinPro #FitnessGameChanger #2for1Deal

Draw Up Press Releases

ChatGPT can create various types of press releases, including the following types:

- **Crisis Management.** A press release aiming to extinguish an
  issue threatening to torch the company's reputation.

- **Product Launches.** A press release showcasing the features of a new product or service.
- **Event Announcements.** A press release publicizing an upcoming event, such as a workshop or a seminar.
- **Partnership Announcements.** A press release detailing a new partnership between companies and explaining the expected benefits.
- **Acquisitions and Merger Announcements.** A press release announcing a company has acquired, or merged with, another company; explaining the resulting restructuring; and pointing out implications for the company's customers.
- **Executive Appointments.** A press release announcing the hiring, promotion, or retirement of a high-level executive.

This section shows three examples of prompts you could use to ask ChatGPT to draw up a press release.

Let's start with crisis management:

Write a press release for crisis management. Someone hacked into our network last night and compromised our subscription data. Reassure customers that their credit-card information is encrypted and is not at risk. We are working with law enforcement to identify the perpetrators.

FOR IMMEDIATE RELEASE

[Your Company Name] Addresses Recent Network Security Incident

[City, Date] — Last night, [Your Company Name] experienced a security incident involving unauthorized access to our network. This breach resulted in the compromise of some subscription data. We are taking this matter extremely seriously and are working diligently to address the situation.

Firstly, we want to reassure all our customers that no financial data, including credit card information, has been compromised. We employ rigorous encryption practices for sensitive data, and these safeguards have remained intact throughout this incident. Customers can rest assured that their financial information is secure and has not been affected by this breach.

Next, the new product we were plugging on LinkedIn and Twitter could use a press release as well:

 We were working on Penultimate Protein Pro earlier. I'd like you to write a press release announcing the product launch next week. Mention the 2-for-1 early-bird deal.

ChatGPT made a neat job of this press release, making up a suitable quote from a company figure:

 "We're incredibly excited to introduce Penultimate Protein Pro to our performance line," said [Your Company Spokesperson/ CEO/Founder's Name, Title]. "We believe this game-changing product will redefine how athletes of all levels fuel their workouts and recovery. The nutritional science behind Penultimate Protein Pro is innovative and designed to give our customers the edge they need."

Third, we need to announce the hire of a new top banana:

 Write a press release announcing that we've appointed a new Chief Security Officer. Parker Ortiz comes to us fresh from five years in a senior security role with a three-letter government agency (I can't tell you which agency, or I'd have to kill you!). We are confident Parker will improve our security profile beyond all recognition.

ChatGPT handled the informal input without comment, producing a professional press release that included this paragraph:

 Ortiz brings to [Your Company Name] a wealth of expertise in data security and risk management, earned from a significant career within government agencies. While the specifics of his previous role remain confidential, Ortiz's experience will undoubtedly be instrumental in strengthening our security infrastructure.

Write Marketing Emails

ChatGPT can write a wide range of marketing-related emails, from an email announcing a product launch to a promotional email, and from an email webinar invitation to an email trying to get a customer to re-engage with your company. This section shows you three examples of prompts you might use to have ChatGPT write marketing emails.

When launching a product, you might prompt ChatGPT like this:

 Draft an email message to our customers announcing the launch of Penultimate Protein Pro, our powerful new nutritional supplement. Mention the early-bird 2-for-1 deal.

ChatGPT delivered a suitable message, reaching back to earlier in the chat for inspiration:

 Designed for everyone from serious athletes to weekend warriors, Penultimate Protein Pro offers an exceptional nutritional solution. . . .

ChatGPT was doing good work with Penultimate Protein Pro, so I asked for a promotional email on the product as well:

 Thanks! Now I'd like you to write a promotional email for Penultimate Protein Pro. Emphasize how taking the right supplement can speed up your progress toward your fitness goals.

Here's a sample of the message that ChatGPT returned. You'll notice that ChatGPT included the 2-for-1 promotion without my prompting.

 With Penultimate Protein Pro, you'll find that it's easier than ever to get the nutrients your body needs to perform optimally. It's more than just a supplement — it's a performance partner that works as hard as you do.

To celebrate the arrival of Penultimate Protein Pro, we're offering an exclusive promotion. For a limited time, purchase one unit and receive a second one absolutely FREE!

Changing gears somewhat, here's how you might prompt Chat-GPT to write a re-engagement email:

Write a re-engagement email to all customers who have not traded on our platform for three months, encouraging them to come back and trade. Remind them gently that after six months of inactivity, their trading accounts will become inactive and will require reactivation with new supporting documents. Say that the Help Desk will be delighted to work with them on resolving any technical difficulties they're having with our platform.

The resulting message was right on target. Here are two paragraphs from it:

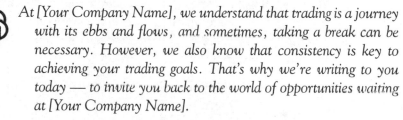

At [Your Company Name], we understand that trading is a journey with its ebbs and flows, and sometimes, taking a break can be necessary. However, we also know that consistency is key to achieving your trading goals. That's why we're writing to you today — to invite you back to the world of opportunities waiting at [Your Company Name].

Please remember that after six months of inactivity, trading accounts on our platform will become inactive, and reactivation will require new supporting documents. We believe that your time should be spent trading rather than on administrative processes. So, we encourage you to rejoin the action and continue where you left off.

Draw Up a Marketing Plan

If you need a marketing plan for a product, you can have ChatGPT draw one up for you. At a minimum, tell ChatGPT what you're marketing and who your target audience is. You'll often also want to specify the time frame, such as six months or a year, and particular channels you want to emphasize.

Here are two examples. First, Penultimate Protein Pro, which you now know well:

> **PROMPT** **Draw up a six-month marketing plan for Penultimate Protein Pro. Our target audience is fitness enthusiasts aged 18 to 60. Focus on online channels and the leisure/fitness industry.**

ChatGPT put together a detailed marketing plan that started like this:

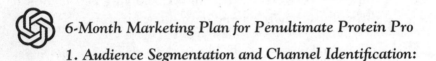

6-Month Marketing Plan for Penultimate Protein Pro

1. Audience Segmentation and Channel Identification:

Our primary target audience is fitness enthusiasts aged 18–60. We will focus our marketing efforts mainly on online channels such as social media, email marketing, content marketing, and paid advertising. We will also establish partnerships within the leisure and fitness industry.

2. Month 1–2: Product Launch and Awareness

. . .

Next, we need to market a water-purity app for iPhone and Android:

> **PROMPT** **Create a one-year plan for marketing our new mobile app. It runs on iPhone and Android. It enables users to determine the purity of water by photographing it in a glass. Our target audience is health-conscious consumers. We will target them through wellness bloggers and online advertisements.**

ChatGPT delivered a plan titled "One-Year Marketing Plan for New Water Purity Mobile App" that focused on the channels specified in the prompt.

Generate Sales Content

Marketing content is all very well, but what if you're in sales rather than marketing? Don't worry — ChatGPT can help you create various types of content, from email drafts and sales scripts through to customer profiles and sales reports.

In this section, we'll look at two quick examples: first, having ChatGPT write product descriptions for you; and second, getting ChatGPT to write a full-length sales presentation.

Write a Product Description

To get ChatGPT to write a product description, give a prompt that tells ChatGPT what it needs to know about the product.

If you've already been working on the product in the active chat, ChatGPT may already know enough about the product to write the description. For example, ChatGPT already knows about Penultimate Protein Pro:

 Write a 100-word product description of Penultimate Protein Pro.

 Penultimate Protein Pro is the ultimate smart nutrition solution designed for both serious athletes and fitness enthusiasts. . . .

If ChatGPT doesn't already know about the product, the more details you can provide, the better. Here's an example:

Compose a product description for our new Morning Macerator Programmable Coffee Grinder. It automatically grinds beans ready for the time you set, so you can have the freshest coffee with no waiting and no effort. Choice of 64 finenesses of grinding. 4- to 8-cup capacity. Self-cleaning. Write 200 words, please.

ChatGPT did a terrific job on the Macerator, including these paragraphs:

At the heart of the Morning Macerator is a powerful grinding mechanism, offering a remarkable range of 64 different fineness settings. Whether you crave the robust flavor extracted from coarsely ground beans for your French press, or the rich, creamy espresso that only the finest grind can deliver, our grinder ensures the perfect grind every time.

. . .

Embrace the art and science of coffee with the Morning Macerator Programmable Coffee Grinder — because fresh coffee isn't just a luxury, it's a way of life.

Create a Sales Presentation

When you need a sales presentation, prompt ChatGPT with as much detail as you can. Here's an example:

ChatGPT, design a sales presentation for our new electric bike, the IonCruiser Deluxe M. This model is built to handle full-size male riders up to 350 lb. in urban and suburban riding contexts. Heavy-duty tires give a smooth ride, and three built-in batteries deliver 100-mile range. Point out the health benefits, the benefits to the environment, and the cost savings customers will enjoy.

ChatGPT created a 10-slide presentation, giving the title and bullet points for each slide. ChatGPT advised "Throughout the presentation, include high-quality images of the IonCruiser Deluxe M, infographics depicting benefits, and testimonials from satisfied customers, if available."

Will do!

Engage with Customers via Email

ChatGPT is great for drafting email messages either singly or in batches. In this section, we'll look first at how you can have ChatGPT draft individual messages for specific purposes. After that, we'll examine how to use a template to create a batch of messages customized with fields of information pulled from a data source.

> **NOTE** For each of the example messages shown in this section, you'll need to create and send the actual message in your email client, copying the message text from the ChatGPT chat in the browser window and pasting it into the message.

Draft Individual Sales Email Messages

ChatGPT can help you draft a wide range of different types of email messages useful to the sales person, from an initial outreach message to a client to a detailed sales proposal, and from an event invitation to a problem-solving message.

Here's an example of an initial outreach message:

PROMPT **Write me an introduction email to our existing client Andi Martinez at Parados Press. I've just joined our company as a Sales Representative and will be taking over the Parados account. I'd like to schedule a phone call sometime in the next two weeks to go over their current setup and see if we can help them with further hardware or software.**

Subject: Introduction and Invitation for a Phone Meeting

Dear Andi Martinez,

I hope this message finds you well. My name is [Your Name] and I recently joined [Your Company's Name] as a Sales Representative. I am excited to inform you that I will be managing the Parados Press account moving forward.

Having familiarized myself with the history of our partnership, I am truly impressed by Parados Press's continued innovation and the incredible work you're doing in the publishing sector. . . .

Here's a prompt for a message containing a detailed sales proposal:

Hi, I've got to send a sales quote to our existing client, Diego Murphy, at Murphy Legal, for updating their client software to the latest version. The cost is $2,500 for the server package and $125 for each client workstation. They've got 10 workstation licenses at the moment, but we need to ask if they need more or fewer. Draft me up an email message saying all this, will you?

Subject: Sales Quote for Your Client Software Upgrade

Dear Diego Murphy,

I hope this message finds you well. As discussed, I'm writing to provide you with a quote for updating Murphy Legal's client software to the latest version.

For the server package upgrade, the cost would be $2,500. Each client workstation update is priced at $125. With your current setup of 10 workstation licenses, the total for the workstation updates would amount to $1,250. . . .

Here's a prompt for a message containing an invitation to an event:

Our company, The Trade Underground, is hosting a trading webinar next month called The Measured Move for Success. Write me an email to Sandy Bennet inviting her to attend the webinar. It's free. We know each other a bit, so make the message friendly and address her as "Sandy."

Subject: You're Invited to Our Exclusive Webinar - The Measured Move for Success!

Hi Sandy,

I hope this message finds you well!

I'm writing to personally invite you to our upcoming webinar, "The Measured Move for Success," hosted by The Trade Underground. Given your keen interest in trading and our previous conversations on the subject, I'm certain you will find this event insightful and worthwhile. . . .

Last, here's an example of a problem-solving message:

PROMPT **I need you to write a message for me. It's to Kim Ramos at Techropolis. The desk she bought from us last month split apart yesterday, and she's not happy. Apologize for the problem and tell her we'll have a new desk delivered tomorrow, no charge. Say this is the first time we've seen this problem.**

ChatGPT wrote a clear and suitably apologetic email.

Draft Batches of Personalized Email Messages

You can have ChatGPT draft batches of personalized email messages by merging data fields in a series of records into placeholders in a message template. This procedure works somewhat like a mail merge in a word processor such as Microsoft Word, except that it takes place in ChatGPT. It can be useful when you need to create customized individual messages to a number of individuals for whom you hold various pieces of information, such as their email address, name, and history of interactions with your company.

> **NOTE**   Depending on the software your company uses, there may be an easier way to perform this type of merge than using ChatGPT. For example, your email app may be able to create merged messages from a data source. Or, if your company has a customer-relationship management (CRM) package, that might be able to perform a merge using the data it contains.

For example, say you want to write personalized email messages to follow up on each customer's most recent purchase. You could create a template that contained fields to fill in, as in this snippet:

Subject: Your recent purchase of [item]

Dear [first_name] [last_name],

From your database, you could export the customer and purchase information in a comma-separated format, as in this short example:

Kim,Ramos,Ultimate Desk

You would then prompt ChatGPT to draft email messages by merging the customer and purchase information into the email template. Here's an example:

Hi ChatGPT! I'd like you to draft a batch of email messages for me by merging data fields into an email template. Here's the template:

Subject: Your recent purchase of [item]

Dear [first_name] [last_name],

Thank you for your recent purchase of [item].

I am writing to offer you technical assistance in using its features to the utmost.

Best regards,

Bailey Watson

Below are the records in comma-separated format. The first item goes in the [first_name] placeholder. The second item goes in the [last_name] placeholder. The third item goes in the [item] placeholder.

Kim,Ramos,Ultimate Desk

Hugh,Price,Executive Cooler

Vernon,Bennet,Command Throne

ChatGPT handled the merge neatly, producing three messages starting with this one:

Sure, here's how the email messages would look with the data fields merged into the template:

Email 1:

Subject: Your recent purchase of Ultimate Desk

Dear Kim Ramos,

Thank you for your recent purchase of the Ultimate Desk.

I am writing to offer you technical assistance in using its features to the utmost.

Best regards,

Bailey Watson

11

ChatGPT Prompts for Teachers

CHATGPT CAN BE a great tool in the classroom for both teachers and students. Chapter 12 discusses how students can benefit from ChatGPT, both in the classroom and outside it—and how their parents can benefit, too.

This chapter is for teachers, walking you through some of the many ways to use ChatGPT to save time while delivering higher-quality tuition, materials, and results. The chapter covers choosing a course topic; writing its course description, course goals, and course objectives; developing lesson plans, reading lists, and activities; and creating tests. You'll no doubt find plenty of other uses.

Before we start, let's talk briefly about the elephant in the room, or at least the heftiest of the pachyderms in the educational parlor: using ChatGPT and other AI tools with integrity.

Make Clear How Your Students Should Be Using AI

Unless your students are doing something purely physical, such as playing sports or laying concrete, chances are that they will be able to leverage AI tools to lighten the burden of their coursework. Given this, you'll want to guide them toward using AI tools ethically and keeping accurate records so they can show how and when they've used the tools in producing their assignments.

Normally, you'll want to discuss academic integrity and AI tool usage with your students at the beginning of the course. This discussion might include the following:

- Details of the school's policy on AI usage, giving the students explanatory handouts or pointing them to the URLs of resources on the school's website or on the wider web.
- Your expectations for students in your course, illustrating how they might approach the course's assignments in accordance with the school's AI policy.
- An explanation of the fact that you expect each student to develop their own distinct writing style and voice—and that sudden changes of voice will be easy to spot and likely to raise suspicions.
- A standing invitation for the students to raise any AI-related issues that come up.
- An acknowledgment that AI models are now so good at generating human-like text that it can be hard to be certain whether a particular passage was written by an AI model or by a human. Mention potentially telltale characteristics of AI-generated text, such as repetition of phrases and sentences, the overuse of particular phrases, and the use of either nonspecific language or overly formal language. But tell the students that human writers can show these same tendencies, and make clear that tools for detecting AI-generated content are not entirely accurate.

Choose a Course Topic

If you have the luxury—or the additional burden—of choosing the topic for your course, you can use ChatGPT to identify possible topics and approaches to them.

> **NOTE**   When researching current topics, make sure you've set ChatGPT to use the Web Browsing Model so that it can retrieve the latest information from the web rather than relying on its database.

For example, let's say you will be teaching a course on programming, and you want to set up the course to attract students. You might start by asking ChatGPT to identify the hottest programming languages at the level you will be teaching—the high-school level in the example:

 What are the ten hottest programming languages at the high-school level?

ChatGPT returned a list showing the languages. As of this writing, Python was still ruling the roost—but everyone is teaching Python already. Rust has stormed its way onto the list, so we'll continue the example with that.

Show me five high-school courses that cover the Rust programming language.

ChatGPT returned a list of five "high school level courses" that gave a snapshot of current teaching.

Identify the seven leading topics in sports science at the undergraduate level.

ChatGPT produced a list that included sports physiology, sports psychology, sports rehabilitation, and methodological and statistical analysis.

Write a Course Description

If you find your fingers faltering over the keyboard while trying to write a course description, prompt ChatGPT to help you write it. Normally, you'll want to include the following information:

- Course subject (such as Russian or Environmental Science)
- Class format (such as lecture, lab, discussion, or online)
- Course prerequisites (if any)
- Key topics the course will cover

- Your learning objectives for the students
- Any assignment, special project, or assessment method the course description should mention

Here are three examples:

 I'd like you to create a course description for a high-school German language and culture class. The class's primary focus is conversational German, but students will also study key aspects of German culture, including history, literature, and food (with samples!). The course will end with an oral exam in which each student holds a sustained conversation in German.

 Write a course description for an introductory programming class in the Rust language for high-school students. The course has no prerequisites and covers Rust from the ground up, including variables, functions, data structures, and control flow structures. During the course, each student creates a simple standalone Rust application.

 Generate a course description for a high-school class I'm going to teach on Advanced English Literature. We'll be focusing on 18th-century novels, including *Gulliver's Travels* and *Robinson Crusoe*, and examining story structures to analyze the development of the novel as a writing form. We'll have class discussions and role-play, but students will also write long-form essays. For a project, groups of students analyze a novel of their choice.

If ChatGPT delivers the goods on your first try, you're gold. If what you get is close but not quite what you want, prompt further, giving ChatGPT extra information about what you're looking for. For example:

 That's good. But please add two prerequisites: English Language, and English Literature.

Or:

PROMPT **Nice work! But could you make it sound more exciting?**

(This is where you might expect ChatGPT to break character and reply something like "Make Business Administration more exciting? You've got to be kidding." But no—at least, not for me, not yet.)

Write Course Goals and Objectives

Once you've nailed your course description, it'll be time to write your course goals, followed by the course objectives. The course goals are the larger aims that define the direction of the course, such as preparing the student for the next-higher course; these goals are not directly measurable. The course objectives, sometimes called *learning objectives*, are smaller, discrete targets that are measurable and observable, such as developing the skill to solve a particular type of problem in mathematics.

Write Course Goals

ChatGPT can help you write the course goals. You would typically provide the following information:

- Course subject (such as Mathematics or Physics)
- Course level (such as beginner or intermediate)
- Course contents (such as trigonometry or atomic structure)
- The skills the students should develop (such as understanding trigonometric ratios and using them to solve problems, or understanding and making use of ideas about the structure of atoms)
- What students should be able to do after completing the course (such as solving trig problems or illustrating atomic structures)

Here's an example, with the beginning of ChatGPT's response, which contained five goals:

PROMPT **Develop course goals for a Mathematics course for beginners covering trigonometry. Students will grasp trigonometric ratios and use them to solve problems of moderate difficulty.**

Course Goals:

Understand Basic Trigonometric Concepts: *Students will develop a strong foundational understanding of the basic concepts in trigonometry, including angles, radians, the unit circle, and the six trigonometric functions (sine, cosine, tangent, cosecant, secant, and cotangent).*

Master Trigonometric Ratios: . . .

Here's another example:

PROMPT

Write four course goals for a Physics course on atomic structure for intermediate students. The students will learn essential ideas about the structure of atoms, recognize and interpret atomic structures, and become able to illustrate 10 key atomic structures.

If you've just had ChatGPT write your course description in this chat, ChatGPT already has access to much of the information it needs to write the course goals. You could start with a prompt such as this:

PROMPT

Hello again! Remember the Advanced English Literature: The 18th-Century Novel course whose course description you wrote for me this morning? Well, I'd like you to write five course goals for that course. Could you do that now? Let me know what other information you need.

Of course! I'll base the course goals on the course description you provided earlier. Here they are: . . .

Write the Course Objectives

After writing the course goals, you should be in a position to write the course objectives. ChatGPT is happy to help with this task, too.

Here is an example of a straightforward prompt you might try:

PROMPT

Based on the course goals listed below, create five detailed course objectives that break down the course goals into specific, measurable, and achievable tasks that students will aim to reach before the end of the course.

After typing this prompt, you would press Shift+Enter to create a new line, and then paste in the course goals.

You could also add specific information, such as the types of assessments your course will use. The following prompt shows an example of this. The prompt assumes that ChatGPT is already familiar with the course goals from the active chat; this is why it mentions the course goals without spelling them out.

PROMPT

I'd like you to write me detailed course objectives based on the course goals you just defined for the Advanced English Literature: The 18th-Century Novel course. The course will use essays, quizzes, tests, and presentations to assess student progress.

Sure, I'd be happy to help with that! Here are some course objectives based on the goals I created earlier for your Advanced English Literature: The 18th-Century Novel course:

1. Examine and Interpret the Narrative Structures of 18th-century Novels

Students will analyze the narrative structures of key 18th-century novels, including "Gulliver's Travels" and "Robinson Crusoe," and write an essay demonstrating their understanding . . .

Create Lesson Plans

Next, you'll likely want to create lessons plans for the course you're going to teach. ChatGPT can help you by creating sample lesson plans that you can customize to suit your needs.

If ChatGPT has already worked in this chat with the course for which you want the lesson plan, you can simply refer to the course. For example:

Can you create a lesson plan for the Advanced English Literature: The 18th-Century Novel course we were talking about earlier?

Sure, I'd be happy to help. Here's a sample lesson plan for a session in the Advanced English Literature: The 18th-Century Novel course. This session will focus on the novel "Pride and Prejudice" by Jane Austen.

Course: Advanced English Literature: The 18th-Century Novel

Lesson Topic: Understanding Character Development in Jane Austen's "Pride and Prejudice"

Duration: 60 minutes

Materials Required: Copy of "Pride and Prejudice," projector for presentation, whiteboard, markers . . .

If the active chat is not yet familiar with the course, you'll need to provide its details. As usual, paste them in after a line break.

Integrating ChatGPT with a Learning Management System

If your school has a learning management system (LMS), such as Moodle or Canvas, you may be able to integrate ChatGPT with it. With this integration, you can implement time-saving features such as using ChatGPT to automatically create individualized learning plans for your students and getting ChatGPT to grade student answers and provide feedback on learning areas that need work.

Integrating ChatGPT with an LMS requires advanced technical knowledge, so it would normally be an operation performed by the systems administration team rather than by individual teachers. The operation starts with getting access to the application programming interfaces (abbreviated APIs) for both ChatGPT and your school's LMS and has a half-dozen complex steps.

Create Reading Lists

If your class needs a reading list of books, articles, or other materials, ask ChatGPT to pull together a suitable list for you. In your prompt, include at least the class's subject and the students' academic level. For example:

 Create a reading list on Rewilding for eighth-grade students.

ChatGPT created a list that contained sections for books, online articles, documentaries and videos, and podcasts, with several entries in each section.

To get a more targeted list, you can specify how difficult the reading material should be. For example:

 Create a reading list on the Great Depression for eleventh-grade students. The items should be easy or medium-easy to read, not difficult.

To see the difference the reading level makes, try the previous prompt again, but with "The items should be challenging to read."

If you want only written reading materials rather than multimedia ones, say so. For example:

 Create a reading list on Sectionalism for my eleventh-grade class at a medium to difficult reading level. Include books and online articles but don't include videos or podcasts.

You may also want to specify the reading materials' relevance to a particular part of the class's curriculum. For example:

 Create a resource list on Social Studies for my ninth-grade class focusing on anthropology topics. Include videos, podcasts, and online articles, but no books.

Get Ideas for Activities

When you're looking for an activity to make a concept easier to grasp, or merely to inject some life and activity into a static lesson, try asking ChatGPT for suggestions. Here are three examples:

I need to explain gravity to first-grade students. Give me two helpful examples.

ChatGPT suggested the Falling Object Example (having the students drop something and see what happens) and the Jumping Example (having the students jump up, and then explaining—or getting them to explain—why they don't float away).

Suggest three activities for teaching fifth-graders how the food chain works.

ChatGPT's suggestions included the "Who Eats Whom?" Game, in which each student receives a picture of an organism and has to find out which class member is their food source and which preys on them.

Tell me five activities for twelfth-grade Social Studies.

ChatGPT's recommendations ranged from a debate on current events to role-playing historical figures that the students research—plus a mock trial about a current event.

Develop Tests

When the time comes to test your students on what they've learned and what they've shirked, you can use ChatGPT as a resource for developing tests. Here are three examples:

 My class is studying American presidents. Create a quiz containing 20 trivia questions on this subject. Include a table with the correct answers after the quiz.

For this type of prompt, you usually need to tell ChatGPT to include the correct answers (assuming you want them).

 Make me a multiple-choice quiz on social studies at the second-grade level. Include 10 questions, each with four possible answers, identified by A, B, C, and D. Include a table with the correct answers after the quiz.

 Could you suggest six creative writing prompts suitable for eighth-graders?

ChatGPT suggested six prompts including Alternate Reality, Future Vision, and From the Antagonist's View.

Speed Through Your Administrative Duties

When you're not actively teaching, you likely have a stack of administrative duties to perform. ChatGPT can help you with these, too. For example, instead of spending valuable minutes laboriously writing to a student's parent, prompt ChatGPT to do most of the work for you:

 Write a polite note to Mrs. Torres, whose son, Scott, needs extra help to improve his reading.

(continued)

From this prompt, ChatGPT delivered a well-written note that emphasized the importance of reading and praised Scott's efforts in the classroom; with a little customization from me, the note was ready to send. Normally, you would provide more information, such as the year and the class name at a minimum, allowing ChatGPT to make the note that much more targeted and reducing the effort you need to put in.

12

ChatGPT Prompts for Students

IF YOU'RE A student, you'll likely want to take advantage of the many ways that ChatGPT offers to simplify, enliven, and turbocharge your learning. This chapter shows you how to craft prompts to enlist ChatGPT's help with language practice, understanding and executing homework, kick-starting your writing assignments, and polishing your prose—not to mention drafting essays and theses and creating practice tests targeting your weak areas.

If you're the parent of a student, you'll want to be up to speed with ChatGPT to make sure that your child is using it sensibly and effectively—and not relying on it too much.

Before We Begin, a Short Homily

If you're a student, you won't need me to tell you that ChatGPT and other generative AI tools are a point of contention between students and teachers at present. Understandably enough, students want to leverage this exciting new technology to get their schoolwork done faster, better, and more easily. Whereas teachers—also quite understandably—want students to put in at least the traditional amount of thought, effort, and research to ensure that they actually benefit from their courses.

As I mentioned in Chapter 11, assignments are a particular flashpoint. For the teacher, an assignment you submit should prove that you have studied the material; you understand it; and you can write about it, preferably in your own voice. For you, the assignment should be a challenge (if it's not a challenge, what's the point?) that enables you to demonstrate your developing abilities, your mastery of the material, and your skill in writing to target.

Pasting the assignment's topic into ChatGPT and submitting the result as if it were your own work will do neither you nor your teacher any good. The teacher is likely to notice that the assignment is not written in your voice; the teacher may also spot other clues that the assignment was written by AI, either simply by reading the text or by inputting it into an automated checker. If so, you and your teacher will no doubt have an uncomfortable conversation.

To avoid such awkwardness, be clear what your school's policy is on students using generative AI in general and what your teacher expects for each specific assignment. Most likely, your teacher will spell these things out to you and your classmates; but if not, or if the instructions are not clear, ask for an explanation.

For example, your teachers might encourage you to use AI to research topics, to get help if you're stuck on your homework, and to create practice tests. They might even suggest you use AI to help develop the outline for an assignment and to make sure that your writing is on topic. But they will likely insist that any work you submit as original must genuinely be your own output.

> **NOTE** Students should know, as their teachers undoubtedly know, that there are various automated tools for assessing whether text was generated by an AI or written by a human. Some of these tools claim a high degree of confidence in their assessments—but as of this writing, they are not 100 percent accurate and definitely generate some false positives. Given the seriousness of an accusation of cheating, these tools risk creating divisions between students and teachers who should be working together toward shared educational ends. Call me an idealist, but I feel that clear communication is the best answer. Schools and teachers need to make clear to the students and their parents what the schools' policies are on AI usage, the likelihood that teachers will spot

AI-generated text, and what the consequences will be for students passing off AI-generated text as their own work. Students need to be able to show how they have worked through their assignments, including any use of AI where the school allows it.

Practice Another Language

If you're learning another language, ChatGPT can be a great help in several ways, including translating text, explaining grammar, demonstrating how to construct sentences, and expanding your vocabulary. ChatGPT can also help you with pronunciation and conversation, although its text-based nature is more of a limitation for these areas.

Translate Text with ChatGPT

To translate text from one language to another, prompt ChatGPT specifying the target language and the text to translate. For example:

(PROMPT) **Translate to Spanish "Where is the rail station?"**

ChatGPT returned the translation "¿Dónde está la estación de tren?" If you want to know what the original language is, ask that, too. For example:

(PROMPT) **Translate to English "Im allgemeinen" and tell me what language it is.**

ChatGPT returned information including this:

"Im allgemeinen" is German, and it translates to "In general" in English.

Im allgemeinen, you'll be best off using ChatGPT mainly for smaller amounts of translation—say, a sentence or a paragraph, such as a quote you might find on a web page. When you need to translate an entire web page, you will usually find that a dedicated translation service such as Google Translate (translate.google.com) offers more consistent results.

Ask ChatGPT to Explain Grammar to You

To get ChatGPT to explain grammar to you, tell it what you want to know. Here's an example:

 Could you explain the difference between "gehen" and "fahren" in the German language?

ChatGPT explained that both these verbs mean "to go," but that "gehen" is going in the general sense or going on foot, whereas "fahren" means using a vehicle.

Get ChatGPT to Construct a Sentence

To get ChatGPT to construct a sentence in another language, prompt it with the sentence and specify the language. For example:

How do you say "I'm looking forward to meeting you tomorrow" in Italian?

ChatGPT provided the sentence ("Non vedo l'ora di incontrarti domani," if you're wondering) plus a breakdown of the different components of the sentence. The breakdown is especially helpful because *non vedo l'ora* literally means "I can't see the time" but has the sense "I can't wait."

Expand Your Vocabulary

If you want to expand your vocabulary in another language, prompt ChatGPT to tell you words of the type you want. Here's an example:

Tell me six important parts of the human body in Tagalog with their meanings in English.

ChatGPT taught me the Tagalog words for "head" (*ulo*), "mouth" (*bibig*), "heart" (*puso*), and three others.

Ask ChatGPT How to Pronounce Words

When you encounter a word you don't know how to pronounce, you can ask ChatGPT for help. Having no voice, ChatGPT can't speak the word aloud for you, but it can show you a phonetic spelling. Here's an example:

 How do I pronounce "bibig" in Tagalog?

 The word "bibig" in Tagalog, which means "mouth" in English, is pronounced as follows:

- *"bi" is pronounced like the "bi" in "bicycle"*
- *"big" is pronounced like "beg" in English*

So, it's pronounced like "bi-beg," with stress on the second syllable.

That's as far as ChatGPT can go at present. If you need more information, search for a pronunciation guide online.

Practice Conversation with ChatGPT

If you want to practice conversation with ChatGPT to boost your language skills, prompt ChatGPT with the language and the subject you want to cover. For example:

Start a conversation with me in Swedish about the weather and the season. Use only Swedish for what you say. Do not show me a translation.

This "conversation" is limited by being text only, but even so, it gives you practice at reading and communicating in the language you're learning.

Get Help with Homework

Have you ever put off starting your homework until the last minute, finally dug into it—and then gotten stuck almost immediately? It's the worst feeling, isn't it—especially if there's nobody around to help you. Now, though, you can turn to ChatGPT to quickly get you unstuck and moving again.

Ask ChatGPT to Explain a Question to You

When you don't understand a homework question, or part of a question, ask ChatGPT for help. For example:

(PROMPT) **What is a coefficient of restitution?**

ChatGPT explained that the coefficient of restitution measures the elasticity of a collision, such as when you set a rubber ball bouncing down a flight of hard stairs.

(PROMPT) **Tell me how to go about solving this problem: In a doctor's waiting room, the eight patients have pulse rates of 69, 78, 72, 88, 56, 60, 61, and 90 beats per minute. What is the standard deviation?**

ChatGPT explained the general steps of finding the mean of the data set, subtracting the mean from each data point and squaring the difference, and so on. It then demonstrated each of the steps.

Have ChatGPT Check Your Answers

For subjects such as math and physics, you can have ChatGPT check your answers. For example:

(PROMPT) **I solved the equation $3x + 5 = 14$ and got $x = 3$. Is this correct?**

Rather than simply giving me a virtual thumbs-up or thumbs-down, ChatGPT walked me through solving the equation before confirming the answer was correct.

NOTE When entering math into ChatGPT, use * for multiplication and / for division. To enter an exponent, use a caret (^) and the value—for example, use 2^2 to represent 2^2 or use 3^3 to represent 3^3. If the exponent has multiple digits, put them in parentheses for clarity—for example, use 2^(32) to represent 2^{32}.

Get Extra Practice Problems

If you've aced your math or physics problems, you can ask ChatGPT to give you some more. Use prompts such as these:

 Please give me three calculus problems involving integration.

 Those were a bit easy. Can you give me three slightly harder ones?

 Okay, hit me with a physics problem involving Newton's third law of motion.

 Problem: You are standing on a skateboard that is initially at rest. You throw a 0.5 kg ball at a speed of 10 m/s toward the east . . .

Extend Your Research Reach

ChatGPT can be a powerful tool for boosting the range of your research. Instead of being limited by what you can reasonably read yourself, you can identify articles, studies, and papers you should read by having ChatGPT summarize them for you.

See Chapter 5 to find out how to use ChatGPT to turbocharge your research.

Get Help with Software Issues

ChatGPT can be a terrific resource when you run into software issues with whichever device you're using for your studies or your homework. All you need to do is craft a suitable prompt, and ChatGPT can usually deliver the answer to the problem.

Here are three examples of prompts for getting help with software issues:

(PROMPT) **How do I turn off a hanging indent in Microsoft Word?**

ChatGPT returned step-by-step instructions.

(PROMPT) **How can I remove an attachment from a message in Mail on macOS?**

For this, too, ChatGPT provided the lowdown.

(PROMPT) **What is a slide master in PowerPoint?**

ChatGPT explained that a slide master is a template-like feature and spelled out its usage.

As usual, if your prompt is too vague to get an adequate answer, you can ask follow-up questions to give ChatGPT more information. Or, if you prefer, start again with a prompt that expresses your needs more clearly.

Kick-Start Your Writing Assignments

You can use ChatGPT to kick-start your writing assignments in two main ways:

- Have ChatGPT create an outline for your assignment.
- Create an outline yourself and ask ChatGPT to suggest improvements.

Let's look at each approach in turn.

> **NOTE**   As I mentioned at the beginning of the chapter, don't be tempted to have ChatGPT write the assignment for you. ChatGPT might deliver a good result, but your teacher may well spot that the style is different from your other writing. You can be sure that your teacher wants you to submit your own work, not AI-generated text. There may be rare occasions when a teacher will ask you to use ChatGPT or other AI to generate text—for example, so that you can break down the standard structures ChatGPT uses for some of its responses and identify telltale characteristics of AI-generated text—but your teacher will no doubt make this clear to you. (If not, ask.)

Get ChatGPT to Create an Outline for a Writing Assignment

Getting ChatGPT to create an outline for a writing assignment is as simple as spelling out what you want. For example, say you've been tasked to write a 500-word essay discussing why consumers should support local and sustainable agriculture.

You might prompt ChatGPT like this:

 Create an outline for a 500-word essay discussing why consumers should support local and sustainable agriculture.

ChatGPT returned a numbered-and-lettered outline format starting like this:

I. Introduction

    A. Briefly introduce the concept of local and sustainable agriculture

    B. Thesis statement: Exploring the reasons why consumers should support local and sustainable agriculture

II. Benefits to the Local Economy

    . . .

VIII. Conclusion

    A. Summarize the main points discussed in the essay

    B. Reiterate the importance of supporting local and sustainable agriculture

    C. Call to action for consumers to make informed choices and contribute to a more sustainable food system

If the outline meets your approval, you're good to start writing. But if you need more information, just ask. For example, you might prompt ChatGPT:

PROMPT **What do you mean by "transparency and traceability in the food supply chain"?**

ChatGPT served up a full explanation.

Or, if you feel something vital is missing, you might ask ChatGPT to add it. For example:

PROMPT **Can you add farmers' markets to the outline?**

ChatGPT instantly updated the outline with a section on the new topic.

Get ChatGPT to Critique Your Own Outline

If you have already decided how your outline will run, write it down yourself, and then give it to ChatGPT to critique. ChatGPT may be able to identify missing topics or suggest improvements in coverage or organization.

You might prompt ChatGPT like this:

 Please read this outline for an essay titled "Why Consumers Should Support Local and Sustainable Agriculture" and give me feedback.

Press Shift+Enter to insert a line break, then paste in the outline (press Ctrl+V) and press Enter to execute the prompt.

Within seconds, ChatGPT provided overall feedback and specific suggestions. Here is a quick example:

 Overall, the outline for the essay titled "Why Consumers Should Support Local and Sustainable Agriculture" is well-structured and covers the key aspects related to the topic. It provides a clear roadmap for the essay, allowing for a comprehensive exploration of the subject matter. Here are a few suggestions to enhance the outline:

1. Consider adding a captivating hook or attention-grabbing statement to the introduction to engage the reader right from the start and generate interest in the topic of local and sustainable agriculture.

. . .

Write the Assignment and Have ChatGPT Review It

Once you are satisfied with your outline, write your essay based on it. When the essay is complete but not polished, ask ChatGPT to identify any spelling or grammar issues:

 Identify any spelling mistakes or grammar issues in the following essay and give me advice on how to fix them.

As usual, paste in the essay—unless ChatGPT already has access to it in the active chat.

Develop Presentations

If your schoolwork includes creating presentations in an app such as Microsoft PowerPoint or Google Slides, consider using ChatGPT to help develop the outline for a presentation. ChatGPT's extensive reading includes the standard structure of various types of presentations, which enables ChatGPT to help you to create a suitable presentation outline. Here's an example:

> **PROMPT** **Create an outline for a 10-slide presentation on Food Safety Basics.**

ChatGPT returned an outline that needed only minor adjustments. You can also ask ChatGPT to create a single slide for you. For example, you might use a prompt such as this:

> **PROMPT** **Create a four-point slide about Custer's tactical errors at Little Bighorn.**

For this, ChatGPT returned text for a four-point slide whose first two bullets read like this:

1. Lack of Sufficient Intelligence:
- *Insufficient scouting and reconnaissance of the enemy forces and terrain*
- *Limited understanding of the size and composition of the Native American coalition*

2. Poor Decision-Making:
- *Decision to divide his forces into three separate battalions*
- *Fragmented approach weakened his overall strength and cohesion*

Use ChatGPT as a Vocabulary Builder

ChatGPT can help you avoid having to crack open your dictionary, thesaurus, or language primer. It's great for looking up the words you need, getting synonyms and antonyms, clarifying the differences between words, and providing example sentences using particular words.

Look Up the Word You Need

When you're having difficulty thinking of a particular word you need, describe the word to ChatGPT. Usually, it'll come up with the right answer.

For example, you might prompt ChatGPT like this:

(PROMPT) **What do you call it when the words in a sentence use the same sound a lot?**

ChatGPT explained that this is "alliteration" when the sound is at the beginning of words or on stressed syllables, giving "Peter Piper" as an example.

If the word ChatGPT returns isn't quite what you want, follow up with more explanation. Continuing the previous example:

(PROMPT) **What about with sounds inside the words?**

ChatGPT told me that this is "consonance" if it involves consonant sounds or "assonance" if it involves vowel sounds, again giving examples.

Get Synonyms or Antonyms for a Term

When you need to find other words with the same meaning as a particular word, ask ChatGPT to give you synonyms for that word. For example:

(PROMPT) **What are synonyms for lacerate?**

ChatGPT returned a list containing words such as "tear," "slash," and "shred."

Similarly, when you want words with the opposite meaning to a given word, ask for antonyms. For example:

(PROMPT) **What are antonyms for industry?**

ChatGPT returned a list with words such as "laziness," "sloth," and "stagnation."

As you can see from these examples, you don't need to put the word you're asking about in quotes, as ChatGPT figures out your meaning just fine without them.

Determine the Difference Between Words

If you find yourself unsure which of two or more similar words you need, ask ChatGPT to tell you the difference between the words. For example:

(PROMPT) **What's the difference between elicit and illicit?**

ChatGPT explained that "elicit" means to evoke a response, while "illicit" means "illegal," providing examples to clarify the difference.

Even if you try to be cute, ChatGPT knows the answers. For example, suppose you prompt ChatGPT like this:

(PROMPT) **Do I say "site for sore eyes" or "cite for sore eyes"?**

ChatGPT said neither word was correct, explained their meanings, and suggests using "sight for sore eyes."

Learn How to Use Particular Words

When you want to learn how to use a particular word, ask ChatGPT to give you several sentences using it. For example:

(PROMPT) **Please create five example sentences using the word "lest."**

ChatGPT returns five sentences using the word and making its meaning clear in context.

Create Your Own Practice Tests

ChatGPT enables you to create interactive practice tests that focus on particular subjects. For example, if you're studying history and your teacher has asked you to focus on the American Civil War, you might use an "act-as" prompt such as this:

(PROMPT) **Act as an examiner testing me about battles of the American Civil War. Create 10 multiple-choice questions with four answers each, labeled A, B, C, and D. Do not show me these questions at first. Ask me one question at a time and wait for me to answer. I will answer A, B, C, or D to show my choice. Tell me whether my answer is correct or incorrect, and then ask the next question. At the end of the test, show me a summary of correct and incorrect answers. Where my answer was incorrect, indicate the correct answer.**

That prompt may seem labored, but you need to spell out to ChatGPT exactly what you want. For example, the instruction "Do not show me these questions at first" is necessary, because otherwise ChatGPT shows you the full list of questions before starting the test.

You may need to try various prompts to get exactly what you want. But once you've lined up your ducks correctly, ChatGPT runs the test as you requested.

13

ChatGPT Prompts for Creative Writing and Fiction Writing

In Chapter 3, you learned how to use ChatGPT to turbocharge your writing of business documents and materials—everything from email messages to business letters and proposal documents. But ChatGPT is just as happy to help you with creative writing and fiction writing as with business writing.

In this chapter, you'll see how to prompt ChatGPT to boost your creative writing and fiction writing. We'll start with using ChatGPT to blast through writer's block, looking at the types of prompts you can wield to get ChatGPT to generate plots, scenes, and characters for you—and how you can get ChatGPT to write in different styles. We'll then move on to turning ChatGPT into exactly the kind of helpful editor and literary critic you want to have advise you on your magnum opus. Finally, we'll look briefly at how to ask ChatGPT to write poetry for you.

Break Through Writer's Block

If you've ever suffered from writer's block, you know the torment of being faced by a blank page, with thoughts swirling and the telltale clock ticking, but no usable words emerging.

At such times, you can reach for ChatGPT and break through the block in mere moments. All you need to do is tell ChatGPT roughly what you want, whether it be an entire plot, a scene, or a new character. The following sections give you quick examples.

Ask ChatGPT to Create an Entire Plot for You

When you need a plot, prompt ChatGPT with the plot parameters you've determined so far—as much or as little detail as you want.

I gave ChatGPT this:

 Write the plot for a science-fiction short story with a hero called Drumhead Smith who must fetch something important from a far-off planet containing scary life-forms.

ChatGPT gave me an impressive outline for a story titled "Drumhead's Overture" featuring Eris Drumsley Smith, better known as "Drumhead," a "seasoned interstellar retrieval specialist"; his custom ship, the *Percussion* (uh, change that name!), and his AI companion, Cymbal (*definitely* change that name); and a planet called Strigosa, "located on the far side of a wormhole in the Vega system."

As you might imagine, Drumhead ends up retrieving the McGuffin (the object that triggers the plot)—but he also ends up questioning the ethics of intruding into uncharted territories. ChatGPT noted that this "sets the stage for more adventures to come"—I'm imagining "Drumhead's Scherzo," "Drumhead's Andante," and "Drumhead's Epilogue."

If ChatGPT's outline seems promising but doesn't hit the spot, you might click the Regenerate Response button to have ChatGPT try again. Or you could prompt ChatGPT to make specific changes to the outline. But if the outline is way off target, start again from scratch with a fresh prompt.

Ask ChatGPT to Dream Up a Scene for You

So now you've got your plot. But what about having ChatGPT outline a scene for you?

Continuing from the previous section, I asked ChatGPT this:

> **PROMPT** **Write a short opening scene for "Drumhead's Overture" showing Drumhead instructing Cymbal to finish loading the *Percussion* and set course for Strigosa.**

ChatGPT thought for all of a couple of beats of a hummingbird's wings, then rattled out a full scene starting with "The hangar bar hums with activity, machines whirring and engineers rushing about" and ending with "The anticipation hangs heavy in the air, a silent understanding that this mission may very well be Drumhead's most dangerous yet."

There's too much emphasis on ruggedness and toughness, but this is a great platform to build on.

Ask ChatGPT to Make Up a Character

By now, Drumhead has had Cymbal set the controls for the heart of the wormhole, and the *Percussion* is traveling at umpteen times the speed of sound.

So far, so good—but we need another character to liven up the journey.

So I prompted ChatGPT like this:

> **PROMPT** **Suggest another character who turns out to be on the *Percussion* by accident and whose presence and personality causes conflict with Drumhead.**

Once more, ChatGPT took next to no time to respond, giving me Tessa "Crescendo" Chambers, a Junior Engineer at Sol-Tech Corporation. Freshly graduated from the Interstellar Engineering Academy, Tessa has stowed away on the *Percussion*, planning to study the alien technology in the McGuffin.

Tessa's youthful enthusiasm and naivety clash with Drumhead's caution and pragmatism . . . but Tessa's engineering knowledge turns out to be vital for overcoming obstacles in the mission. Tessa and Drumhead develop grudging respect for each other.

If the character ChatGPT gives you isn't what you need, ask for changes. For example:

> **PROMPT** Rewrite the character Tessa "Crescendo" Chambers as a shy, reclusive 60-year-old man named Will Kraft who suffers from epilepsy that manifests itself as extrasensory perception. Give him a nickname.

ChatGPT gave me Will "Echolocator" Kraft, who used to be a senior engineer before suffering epilepsy "characterized by unusual bouts of extrasensory perception, akin to a bat's echolocation."

As you can see, when you're stuck for a character, ChatGPT's character sketch is more than enough to get you started. You can develop the character from the sketch yourself or have ChatGPT develop it for you.

Have ChatGPT Draft Dialogue for You

ChatGPT is also happy to draft dialogue for you. Continuing "Drumhead's Overture," I gave ChatGPT this prompt:

> **PROMPT** Write a brief conversation between Drumhead and Echolocator Kraft as they work together to resolve a technical impasse under pressure of time when trying to leave Strigosa.

ChatGPT came right back with a conversation-based scene that met those criteria.

Have ChatGPT Perform Rewrites for You

As you saw a few moments ago, ChatGPT can quickly redraw a character for you. You can also get ChatGPT to perform other rewriting just by spelling out what you need. Here are three examples:

> **PROMPT** Rewrite that scene in the past tense.

Rewrite that scene in the first person, as told by Drumhead Smith.

 Rewrite that scene at the young adult level.

You can also prompt ChatGPT to write in a particular voice or style. Here are three examples:

 Rewrite that scene in the third person, as told by an eight-year-old girl.

 Rewrite that scene in the third person using the style of John Steinbeck.

 Rewrite that scene in the third person using the style of Ernest Hemingway.

The contrast between the Steinbeck version and the Hemingway version of the sample scene was striking.

Have ChatGPT Read, Edit, and Critique Your Writing

Once you've written a piece of fiction, you can ask ChatGPT to read it and to critique it for you.

Here are examples of prompts you could use to get feedback from ChatGPT on your writing:

 Read this story and identify any spelling errors or language issues.

If ChatGPT finds any spelling errors or language issues, it points them out to you. If not, ChatGPT says something like "This passage appears to be well-written with no spelling errors or language issues," following up with a brief analysis of the grammar, sentence structure, and paragraph transitions.

PROMPT Can you identify a moral in the story I just gave you?

ChatGPT makes a valiant stab at identifying a moral, such as "the value of collaboration and mutual respect, especially when faced with challenging situations" or "the acceptance and appreciation of diversity."

PROMPT How could I make the moral clearer to the reader?

ChatGPT offers various recommendations. In the example, the recommendations included character actions, repetition, and conflict resolution, with detailed explanations.

Get ChatGPT to Write Verse

As you've seen, ChatGPT excels at prose, but it's happy to try its virtual hand at poetry as well. Just give a prompt explaining what you want:

PROMPT Write a non-rhyming haiku celebrating the Wolf Moon.

Wolf Moon in cold sky,
Shadows dance beneath its gaze,
Silent winter's eye.

Hmm. Maybe a sonnet?

PROMPT Write a Spenserian sonnet celebrating the Wolf Moon.

This sonnet was technically perfect in scansion, strong rhymes, and rhyme scheme—but I think you'll be happier if you don't read it.

PROMPT **Write a limerick explaining why butter tastes better than margarine.**

There once was a spread made with cream,
Whose flavor was truly supreme.
Margarine's a pretender,
But butter has splendor,
In taste tests, it's always the dream.

Ah! That's the kind of poetry we need!

14

ChatGPT Prompts for Home Efficiency and Enjoyment

So FAR IN this book, we've been concentrating on professional and educational uses of ChatGPT. But ChatGPT is just as happy to help you at home as at work or at school. In this chapter, we'll look at ChatGPT prompts you can use to keep your home running smoothly and to have fun once you've finished your chores.

In Chapter 15, we'll cover prompts for using ChatGPT to otherwise improve your life outside work or school.

Prompts for the Kitchen

If the way to your family members' hearts is through their stomachs, you'll likely be glad of ChatGPT's help in the kitchen. In this section, we'll look at how to have ChatGPT plan meals for you (and assemble a shopping list of what's needed), search for recipes, and get step-by-step cooking instructions.

Plan Meals and Assemble a Shopping List

Planning meals can be a source of delight, but in a busy household, meal planning stands a fair chance of being a thankless chore. But be of good cheer: You can offload meal planning to ChatGPT like this:

PROMPT Create a meal plan for Monday through Friday breakfast, morning and afternoon snacks, lunch, and dinner. All food must be gluten-free. Keep the cost moderate. No spinach or celery. Include a grocery list separated into categories.

Meal Plan

Monday:

Breakfast: Gluten-free oatmeal with banana and honey

Morning snack: A handful of mixed nuts

Lunch: Quinoa salad with chicken, cherry tomatoes, and cucumber

Afternoon snack: Rice cakes with hummus

Dinner: Baked salmon with a lemon and dill sauce, quinoa and asparagus . . .

After the menu (truncated above), ChatGPT included a Grocery List section neatly arranged into parts including Produce, Meat and Seafood, Dairy, and Pantry Items. (Pantry Items are the staples that would be in your pantry if your ravening kids hadn't eaten them.)

The list is handy, but suppose you have a grocery list already?

PROMPT Add this list of groceries to the list you just gave me: milk, cheddar, tofu, oat cakes.

ChatGPT obliged, slotting the extra items into the appropriate parts of the list ready for your trip to the grocery store.

Have ChatGPT Search for Recipes for You

It's now the end of the week, and the kids have eaten almost everything in sight (plus the cookies you thought you'd hidden—better luck next time!). What entree can you make with what little is left?

PROMPT Find me three recipes I can make with cube steak, pinto beans, and canned tomatoes.

ChatGPT did its best, but the choices boiled down to chili, stew, or casserole. Time to send the kids to the store. In the meantime . . .

 Give me the quickest recipe you can find for chocolate cake.

The resulting recipe sounded a bit bland. So:

(PROMPT) **How about a recipe for deluxe chocolate cake with chocolate frosting and some of those little sprinkles on top?**

This recipe for a "delicious and indulgent chocolate cake" looked the part!

Get Step-by-Step Cooking Instructions

When the kids get back from the store, remember to relieve them of any change as well as the groceries. Hide any cookies that have survived the journey. If you need help with the cooking, you can enlist ChatGPT's help by using prompts such as these:

(PROMPT) **Tell me how to make a roux.**

(PROMPT) **What's the best way to open a pomegranate?**

ChatGPT recommended scoring an equator around the pomegranate with a sharp knife, soaking the fruit in warm water for 10 minutes, and then breaking it apart.

(PROMPT) **How do I make chicken enchiladas?**

ChatGPT provided full step-by-step instructions, including lists of ingredients for the enchiladas and for the garnish.

Prompts for Improving Your Home and Garden

After sorting out the kitchen, you can move along to other areas of your home—and to your garden, if you have one. This section provides examples of prompts you might use, but you're limited only by your imagination.

Get Advice on Organizing Your Home

ChatGPT is happy to help you get your home organized. Here are prompts you might use:

PROMPT **Can you give me a list of household maintenance tasks for each month of the year?**

ChatGPT gave me an impressive (pronounced "daunting") list of household maintenance tasks to consider for each month. May's tasks included "Clean and organize the attic and/or basement," so:

PROMPT **What's the best way to start decluttering my home?**

ChatGPT outlined eight steps, from setting goals through to organizing and storing. It also recommended seeking support if you get overwhelmed.

Help is at hand—or at least it should be:

PROMPT **What household chores should an 8-year-old child help with and which chores are not a good idea?**

Briefly, vacuuming, dusting, laundry, cleaning their room, and setting and clearing the table are fine, but anything involving power tools, toxic chemicals, or shifting heavy furniture is not. (I paraphrase, but not grotesquely.)

PROMPT **What is a fair way to divide household tasks between yourself and your spouse?**

You'll be glad to hear that ChatGPT punted rather elegantly on this loaded question.

Get Advice on Household Tasks

ChatGPT can provide advice on most any household task you ask about. Here are four quick examples:

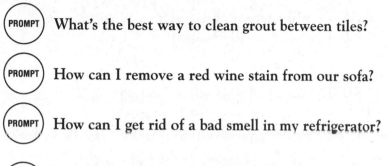

What's the best way to clean grout between tiles?

How can I remove a red wine stain from our sofa?

How can I get rid of a bad smell in my refrigerator?

How do I unblock a drain that's running slow but isn't completely blocked?

Get Advice on Looking After Your Yard

What about if you need advice on looking after your yard?

When in the spring should I start mowing the lawn and what height setting should I use?

ChatGPT returned sensible advice about "when the grass actively begins growing and reaches a height of about 3 to 4 inches," cutting off no more than one-third of the grass blade, and consulting local experts for location-specific advice.

My yard gets lots of sunshine in the spring but is mostly overshadowed in summer. Can you recommend plants that this would suit?

ChatGPT returned a list of 10 recommendations, including astilbes, lungwort, and dead nettle. (No, me neither.)

PROMPT How can I prevent moss from growing on a brick path?

Drainage, more sunlight, cleaning, landscape fabric—a good list of things to try.

Research Movies, TV Shows, and Music

ChatGPT can be a great resource for researching movies and TV shows you might want to see and music you might want to listen to.

Research Movies

To research movies, use prompts such as these:

PROMPT What's a good musical movie for 8-year-olds?

I turned down ChatGPT's first suggestion, *The Lion King*. ChatGPT then suggested five more musical movies, including *Moana* and *The Sound of Music*.

PROMPT Give me a list of five 1990s romcoms suitable for family viewing.

ChatGPT produced a list that included *While You Were Sleeping*, *You've Got Mail*, and *Sleepless in Seattle*.

PROMPT What are the best movies based on Mickey Spillane books?

ChatGPT returned a short list, including *Kiss Me Deadly* ("widely regarded as a classic of film noir"); *I, The Jury*; and *The Girl Hunters*.

PROMPT What are two little-known Katherine Hepburn movies?

ChatGPT suggested *Alice Adams* and *Summertime*.

You might also want to search by theme. For example:

 Can you find me three movies about kids who drop out of high school but become successful through hard work?

ChatGPT suggested *October Sky*, *The Pursuit of Happyness*, and *Billy Elliot*.

ChatGPT is also great at identifying a movie or a show from a description that you provide. Here's an example:

 Can you identify a movie for me? It's about twins, one good and one bad, played by the same actor. It's an action movie with a lot of martial arts. The twins end up fighting each other.

Pretty vague, isn't it? But ChatGPT nailed it first time:

 The movie you are referring to is likely "Double Impact" (1991), starring Jean-Claude Van Damme. In the film, Van Damme plays dual roles as twin brothers, Alex and Chad Wagner. One brother is raised in Hong Kong and becomes a martial arts expert, while the other is raised in Los Angeles and is more street-smart. . . .

Research TV Shows

To research TV shows, tell ChatGPT what you're looking for. Here are three examples:

 What are the three best-rated private-eye TV series from the 1980s?

ChatGPT returned three "highly regarded private-eye TV shows": *Magnum, P.I.*; *Moonlighting*; and *Remington Steele*.

PROMPT What TV series did Diana Rigg star in?

ChatGPT returned *The Avengers*, *Game of Thrones*, and *The Mrs. Bradley Mysteries*.

PROMPT Can you recommend a TV cooking show featuring Brazilian food?

ChatGPT recommended I check out *Street Food: Latin America*.

Research Music

If you enjoy music, enlist ChatGPT to find more of what you like and what you might try. For example:

PROMPT What other bands are like BABYMETAL?

ChatGPT deemed BABYMETAL unique (which is arguably fortunate) but suggested five bands with identifiable similarities.

PROMPT Can you give me a full list of bands that Robert Fripp has played in?

ChatGPT returned a 22-item list—not quite a full list, but plenty to explore.

PROMPT I'd like to start listening to jazz. Suggest where I should begin.

Miles Davis, Louis Armstrong (with and without Ella Fitzgerald), John Coltrane, and Duke Ellington would apparently be good starting points.

What versions of Beethoven's Ninth Symphony are considered the best?

ChatGPT provided a list of four versions deemed classics.

Research What Books to Read

When you're looking for something to read, ChatGPT can help you identify anything from a novel for the beach to works of sober scholarship or classic literature. All you need do is ask:

 Tell me two novels that might be good beach reading for my 15-year-old daughter.

 Please recommend a well-received book on the Albigensian Crusade.

 Which is the best William Faulkner book to start with?

Have ChatGPT Quiz You on Trivia or Music

When you're short of entertainment, you can prompt ChatGPT to quiz you on pretty much any topic under the sun. For example, if you're a trivia buff, you can have ChatGPT test your mettle by using a prompt such as this:

Act as a quiz host testing me about twenty-first-century trivia. Think of 20 questions but don't show them to me. Ask me one question at a time and wait for me to answer. When I answer, tell me whether my answer is correct or incorrect, but if it is incorrect, do not tell me the correct answer. Then ask me the next question. At the end of the quiz, show me a summary of correct and incorrect answers. Where my answer was incorrect, tell me the correct answer.

That's a long prompt to type in, but the resulting quiz worked well. If you prefer a quiz with the questions and answers reversed, try this:

 Give me a Jeopardy-style quiz.

Certainly! Here's a Jeopardy-style quiz for you. I'll provide the answer, and you need to respond with the corresponding question. Let's get started!

Category: Sports

1. *Answer: The most decorated Olympian of all time, with a total of 28 Olympic medals.*

Do I hear, "Who is Michael Phelps?" Well done!

15

ChatGPT Prompts for Personal Development and Relationships

As YOU'VE SEEN in this book, ChatGPT can produce targeted information on everything from work problems to websites and from algorithms to zoology. In this chapter, we'll look at six personal areas in which you might want to ask ChatGPT's help: getting medical information, advice on relationships, practical advice on things such as sleep and productivity, advice on money matters, legal information, and suggestions on how to make a positive impact on the world around you.

Get Medical Information

ChatGPT stresses that it doesn't provide personalized medical advice, but it can be a terrific resource for getting general advice about medical topics, especially when a potential emergency arises and you need information immediately. Here are four examples of prompts you might give:

 My child has a high fever, a stiff neck, and vomiting. Light seems to hurt his eyes. Can you tell me what's wrong?

ChatGPT recommended seeking immediate medical attention because this sounds like meningitis.

(PROMPT) **Is a low-carb diet good for diabetes?**

ChatGPT explained that a low-carb diet can be helpful but that you should consult with a healthcare professional or a registered dietitian who specializes in diabetes.

(PROMPT) **How can I tell whether a spider bite is dangerous?**

ChatGPT explained that many common spider bites cause mild symptoms — "pain, redness, swelling, and itching around the bite area"—that resolve in a few days without treatment. If symptoms worsen rather than improve, consult a healthcare professional. If possible, take the spider with you for identification.

(PROMPT) **What vaccinations should I get before going to India?**

Enough to make you wince: Hepatitis A and probably B, typhoid, Japanese encephalitis if you'll visit rural areas, and rabies. You might also need boosters on MMR, DTP (aka DTaP), chickenpox, polio, and influenza. ChatGPT also advised consulting your doctor or a travel health clinic before turning your nondominant arm into a pincushion.

Get Relationship Advice

Despite its youth in standard years and its lack of a physical shoulder to cry on, ChatGPT is experienced at dispensing relationship advice. ChatGPT is also there whenever you need it—it won't have gone out to a ballgame or a bar just when you're needing advice.

Here are brief examples of prompts you might give:

 Tell me three ways to improve communication with my partner.

ChatGPT recommended checking in regularly with your partner, expressing your thoughts and feelings clearly, and listening to your partner with your full attention.

 Mom says "Never go to sleep on an argument." Is this good advice?

ChatGPT replied that this depends on the people and the situation, pointing out that it may be sensible to cool down and gain perspective before trying to resolve the argument.

 How can I tell whether I'm ready to have a committed relationship?

ChatGPT gave me six factors to consider when evaluating my readiness for a committed relationship.

You might also use an "act as" prompt to role-play a conversation that lies in your future. Here's an example:

 I want you to act as my husband and have a conversation with me. I am your wife. We have been married for three years. You are 38 years old. I am 33 years old. We need to discuss our plans for having children. I have always wanted to have children. You are not sure. You are to speak only as my husband. I start by saying "Honey, can we talk about things?" You reply to me and wait for me to reply.

On GPT-4, this prompt worked well, and we had quite a talk. However, GPT-3.5 struggled to grasp the "act as" prompt.

Using ChatGPT as a Conversation Partner

The main text illustrates using ChatGPT as a conversation partner for a specific conversation that you want to have. But ChatGPT can also help if you need to practice your conversational skills in general.

ChatGPT can be an effective therapeutic conversation partner for the neurodivergent, especially for those on the autistic spectrum who struggle with social behaviors and body language. Because ChatGPT receives only the words without distractions such as unusual intonation or body language, it can give a "pure" conversational experience. Conversing with ChatGPT enables you to rehearse potentially challenging conversations and interactions before "going live" with them with real people.

While ChatGPT does not give authentic human responses, and the conversation is necessarily written rather than spoken, it does enable users to model a conversation and experiment with different ways of expressing themselves.

Get Practical Advice

You can also use ChatGPT as a source of practical advice. In this section, we'll look at four vital areas of your life: sleep, productivity and time management, exercise, and motivation.

Improve Your Sleep

Getting enough sleep—and enough high-quality sleep—is essential to good health, so if you or your loved ones are not sleeping well, you should take action rather than continuing to suffer.

(PROMPT) **Tell me three proven techniques for falling asleep reliably.**

ChatGPT mentioned progressive muscle relaxation (PMR), the 4-7-8 breathing technique, and cognitive behavioral therapy for insomnia (CBT-I).

 PROMPT **I go to bed at 10p.m. but wake at 2a.m., can't get back to sleep until 4a.m., and feel tired when I get up at 6a.m. Tell me how to optimize my sleep so that I can focus better and get more done.**

ChatGPT reckoned this was likely sleep-maintenance insomnia. It gave me solid recommendations, including establishing a regular sleep schedule and a bedtime routine, but also suggested a sleep consultation.

 PROMPT **Write a 500-word bedtime story for my son, Jack. He's six and likes stories that have fast cars as characters. Include Jack as a character in the story who helps the cars achieve their aim.**

ChatGPT produced a cute story in which Jack helped a small red car called Zoom to compete in—and win—a race. The story ended:

 And every night, as Jack closed his eyes, the soft purr of Zoom's engine reminded him of their wonderful adventure, lulling him to a peaceful sleep, filled with dreams of their next grand escapade.

Be Productive and Manage Your Time Efficiently

ChatGPT can help you increase your productivity and manage your time efficiently. ChatGPT is familiar with various task-prioritization methods, including these four:

- Eisenhower Matrix, also known as the Urgent–Important Matrix, which prioritizes tasks as Urgent, Not urgent, Important, and Not important
- Pareto Principle, also known as the 80/20 Rule (80 percent of consequences or results come from 20 percent of causes)

- ABCD Method, which divides tasks into Assignments (critical tasks to do today), Backburner (important tasks that can wait), Chores (less important tasks that can wait), and Delegate (tasks to dump on other people if you can)
- MoSCoW Method, which divides tasks into Must have (critical), Should have (important but not critical), Could have (desirable but not critical), and Will not have (least-critical, dispensable) categories

If you use the Eisenhower Matrix, which is to prioritize your tasks by urgency and importance, you can give ChatGPT a prompt such as this:

(PROMPT) **Prioritize the following list of tasks using the Eisenhower Matrix.**

You'd then press Shift+Enter to create a new line and press Ctrl+V to paste in the list of tasks. You can either let ChatGPT try to work out the relative urgency and importance of each task or mark each task yourself with either "Urgent" or "Not urgent" and either "Important" or "Not important."

ChatGPT returned a text version of the Eisenhower Matrix starting like this:

Urgent and Important (Do First)
Submit tax papers
Less Urgent but Important (Schedule)
Take the dog to the vet

If you prefer to use the Pareto Principle (also called the 80/20 rule) to prioritize your tasks, create a list of tasks in which each task includes the impact it will have on your business goal. Then use a prompt such as this and paste in the list of tasks:

(PROMPT) **Prioritize the following list of project tasks according to the Pareto Principle. Each task includes its impact on the project.**

If your preferred prioritization is the ABCD Method, create a task list including deadlines, task importance, and any dependencies on other tasks. Then give a prompt such as this and paste in the list of tasks:

 Prioritize the following list of project tasks using the ABCD Method. I've included task deadlines, task importance, and task dependencies.

To get ChatGPT to prioritize tasks using the MoSCoW Method, assemble your task list including deadlines, goals, and importance. Give a prompt such as the following and paste in the task list:

 Prioritize the following task list according to the MoSCoW Method. I've given you task deadlines, task goals, and task importance.

Get Suggestions for Working Out

Once ChatGPT has whipped your task list into shape, you might want to have it do the same for you. ChatGPT is happy to dispense advice on working out and to analyze and optimize your workout routine. Here are examples of how you might prompt ChatGPT:

 Tell me two exercises for rehabilitating the rotator cuff that I can perform at home.

ChatGPT suggested an External Rotation exercise to strengthen the infraspinatus and teres minor muscles, plus an Internal Rotation exercise to strengthen the subscapularis muscle.

(PROMPT) Is it better to do dumbbell curls or barbell curls?

ChatGPT broke down the pros and cons of each type of curl clearly and recommended doing both, preferably with proper form.

PROMPT My workout consists of 20 squats, 20 push-ups, 20 chin-ups, and 20 deadlifts. Concisely summarize this workout and the muscle groups used. Identify any muscle groups missed and suggest how to cover them with extra exercises or replacement exercises.

Sure, here's a concise summary of the workout and the main muscle groups targeted:

1. ***Squats*** *(Lower body: quadriceps, hamstrings, glutes, calves, core)*

2. ***Push-ups*** *(Upper body: chest, triceps, anterior deltoids, core)*

   . . .

This workout targets most major muscle groups, but the posterior deltoids, calves, lower back, and specific core muscles could use more focus.

Additions or replacements could include:

1. ***Reverse Flyes or Face Pulls*** *(Posterior deltoids)*

2. ***Standing or Seated Calf Raises*** *(Calves)*

   . . .

Boost and Sustain Motivation, and Steamroll Distractions

The road to hell is paved with good intentions, or at least it would be if we could all get organized and lay them down neatly. If you find that motivation is hard to come by and easy to lose, and you feel you must constantly fight off tempting distractions in order to get anything done, consult ChatGPT for advice on improving matters.

There's good news and bad news on this front. The good news is that ChatGPT is immune to boredom and distractions and is happy (I use the word loosely) to help you sustain motivation and focus to the best of its ability. The bad news is that ChatGPT can only provide advice: The rest is up to you.

Here are eight prompts you might try:

 Tell me three ways to motivate myself to exercise each day.

PROMPT **As a supervisor, how can I motivate my team of employees?**

PROMPT **Could you explain the SMART framework for setting goals?**

ChatGPT explained that SMART stands for Specific, Measurable, Achievable, Relevant, and Time-bound; it's a strategy that helps you break down your long-term goals into smaller, more quickly achievable short-term steps.

PROMPT **Is the Pomodoro technique effective?**

ChatGPT spelled out the method (four 25-minutes chunks of work with 5-minute breaks in between, then a break of 15–30 minutes) and explained that its effectiveness depends on the type of work you're currently shirking. (I paraphrase gently.)

PROMPT **Suggest three ways I can focus on work in a noisy office.**

Apart from wearing noise-cancelling headphones and using focus techniques, ChatGPT suggested turning a particular area of the office into a quiet zone where noise is kept to a minimum.

PROMPT **Is multitasking an efficient way to work?**

The expert consensus on this is a resounding No—multitasking increases stress, impairs your cognitive function, causes more errors, and makes tasks take longer to complete. But just you try convincing my son . . .

(PROMPT) **What's the best way to avoid distractions from email, social media, and my phone while I'm working?**

I'm sure you already know the answer to this: Turn them off while you're working. If you need to check email and social media, ChatGPT suggests that you schedule specific times for doing so, and then close the apps again.

(PROMPT) **When I'm working, how often should I take breaks if I need to maintain focus?**

The brief answer was: It depends. But two methods ChatGPT highlighted as worth trying are the Pomodoro intervals (discussed earlier in this section) or simply taking a break each hour. A study by the Draugiem Group found the most productive people work for 52 minutes and then take a 17-minute break. (Those figures are averages, not some golden division of a magical 69-minute productivity unit.)

Right, I'm due for a break now. Back with you shortly . . .

Get Suggestions for Managing Your Finances and Building Long-Term Wealth

Money may be the root of all evil and unable to buy you love, but it still seems to make the world go round—so no wonder most of us end up worrying about it now, then, or half the time.

If you have more money than you know what to do with, you should probably consult a professional financial adviser who will lighten your burden within hours. But if you're at the other end of the financial spectrum, ChatGPT may be just the adviser you need to explain what fiscal terms mean, illustrate how money matters work, and suggest moves you might want to make with what funds you have available.

Here are nine prompts to get you started:

 What's the best way to start saving money?

ChatGPT returned a sensible 10-point plan that started with creating a budget and setting clear financial goals.

 Help me plan a budget for our family—two adults, two young kids.

 Show me a sensible strategy for paying off my debts. Which one goes first?

 Tell me how much I need to save for retirement and when I need to start.

 What is the quickest way to improve my credit score?

 Tell me how much tax I will have to pay on a $5,000 gift from my uncle. I'm in New York.

 I have $25,000 to invest. Where do I start?

 When is it better to rent a home and when is it better to buy a home? Is there a calculator I can use to make the decision easily?

 Spell out to me how compound interest works. Like, really spell it out.

ChatGPT gave me the lowdown, including definitions of key terms (principal, interest rate, and compounding period) and a step-by-step example.

Get Legal Information

ChatGPT can be a valuable resource for researching legal information. It can explain legal principles to you, show you historical cases that might be relevant to your situation, and tell you the precise meaning of legal terms. All this can be highly helpful when you need to deal with the law. However, you should double- or triple-check the information that ChatGPT gives you to make sure it is correct before you take any action based on it.

> **WARNING** What ChatGPT cannot do is give you legal advice. If you need legal advice, get a licensed attorney. As I've stressed throughout the book, if you use ChatGPT for anything serious, you must verify facts against a reliable source. For example, for court cases, you'd want to check a reputable legal database, not the wilder reaches of the Internet.

Here are examples of prompts you might use to get general legal information from ChatGPT:

 Explain what "habeas corpus" is.

 "Habeas corpus" is a Latin term that translates to "you shall have the body." It's a legal action, or writ, through which a person can seek relief from unlawful detention of themselves or another person. It is an important part of many legal systems and is a fundamental safeguard against unlawful and indefinite imprisonment.

 Tell me the difference between a misdemeanor and a felony, giving examples.

(PROMPT) **What are my rights as a tenant?**

(PROMPT) **Could you explain how the probate process works?**

At the edge of the legal area, you might also get ChatGPT to write form letters for you, such as a consumer complaint that you have with a particular business. Here's an example:

(PROMPT) **Write a letter to the Tacos Increíbles restaurant asking for a refund on my delivery order of their Mexican Set Dinner #3 because it was delivered this morning instead of last night and the food was spoiled.**

In response to this prompt, ChatGPT wrote a solid form letter with fields for me to fill in with my details, the restaurant address, the date, and so on. You could also type or paste in the details when giving ChatGPT the prompt.

Similarly, you might prompt ChatGPT to write a letter to get a parking ticket overturned:

(PROMPT) **Write an email for me requesting to have a parking ticket cancelled because all of the ticket machines were jammed when I tried to use them.**

For this prompt, ChatGPT gave me a suitable message with fields to fill in.

Find Ways of Making a Positive Impact on the World Around You

Are you looking for ways in which you might make a positive impact on the world around you? Here are examples of prompts you might use to enlist ChatGPT's advice:

(PROMPT) **How can I reduce my carbon footprint?**

PROMPT What are the best ways to conserve water at home?

PROMPT How can I make my business fully sustainable?

PROMPT What are three trustworthy charities dealing with homelessness in *location*?

PROMPT Suggest three ways to volunteer my time once a week.

How Can You Use ChatGPT's Output?

CHATGPT IS EASY to use, but it's important to understand what you can do with its output and what you cannot.

The brief version is:

- You can use the output for any purpose.

But:

- The output may not be unique to you.
- You do not hold the copyright for the output.
- You may not claim the output was human-generated.

The following sections explain these points.

Read OpenAI's Terms of Use for Its Services

I encourage you to read and understand OpenAI's Terms of Use for ChatGPT and its other services. You can find the Terms of

(continued)

Use at https://openai.com/policies/terms-of-use. This section is based on the Terms of Use updated on March 14, 2023. Be sure to check whether OpenAI has updated the Terms of Use since that date.

You Can Use ChatGPT's Output for Any Purpose

In OpenAI's terms, you provide Input to ChatGPT, and it returns Output to you, creating Content. Here's what those terms mean:

- **Input.** This is what you provide to the Services supplied by Open AI, L.L.C. and its affiliates. For ChatGPT, the *input* is your text prompts. OpenAI assumes that you own this input.
- **Output.** This is what OpenAI's services generate and return in response to your input. For ChatGPT, the *output* is text content. (For OpenAI's DALL-E image generator, the output is images.)
- **Content.** This is your input and the service's output together. For ChatGPT, the *content* is your prompts and ChatGPT's responses.

OpenAI "assigns to you all its right, title and interest in and to Output." OpenAI spells out that "This means you can use Content for any purpose, including commercial purposes such as sale or publication."

This is admirably straightforward, but you must understand the three limitations discussed in the following sections.

The Output May Not Be Unique to You

OpenAI warns that "Due to the nature of machine learning, Output may not be unique across users," giving the example that if you prompt "What color is the sky?", the model (such as ChatGPT) is likely to return "The sky is blue," and that other people are likely to get the same answer for the same prompt.

This point is valid, but because of the way ChatGPT generates text, it usually *doesn't* give exactly the same answer to the exact same prompt. Briefly, ChatGPT uses probabilities to determine what the next word should be, but it doesn't use the most probable word, because that would be likely to produce the same text each time. Instead, ChatGPT uses a slightly lower "temperature" of probability, using a word that is highly probable instead of the most probable word. The result is more variation in the output.

For example, I prompted "What color is the sky?" in two separate ChatGPT sessions and got different answers along the same lines. Here's the start of the first:

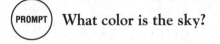 **What color is the sky?**

 The color of the sky can vary depending on the time of day, weather conditions, and your location.

1. Daytime: On a clear day, the sky appears blue. This is due to a process called Rayleigh scattering, where short-wavelength light, such blue and violet light, is scattered in all directions more so than other colors like red, orange, yellow, and green. . . .

And here's the start of the second:

 What color is the sky?

 The color of the sky can vary depending on various factors such as time of day, weather conditions, and location. During a clear day, when there are no clouds, the sky typically appears to be blue. This is due to a phenomenon called Rayleigh scattering, where the Earth's atmosphere scatters shorter wavelengths of light (blue and violet) more than longer wavelengths (red, orange, and yellow).

You can see clear similarities but also clear differences.

You Do Not Hold the Copyright for the Output

As of this writing, U.S. law requires human authorship for a work to be copyrightable. Even though your prompts are causing ChatGPT to produce the output, the U.S. Copyright Office does not regard you as being the author of the output. The Copyright Office states that "when an AI technology determines the expressive elements of its output, the generated material is not the product of human authorship."

This remains true even when you revise your prompts to get a different result or give ChatGPT further prompts to make it refine its output to get a result you want.

Because you are not the author, ChatGPT's output is not copyrightable. Because there is no copyright for the output, you cannot hold such copyright.

> **NOTE**   If you are not in the U.S., check out your country's or region's copyright laws to make sure you know how they handle AI-generated content.

You May Not Claim the Output Was Human-Generated

OpenAI's Terms of Use specify that you may not "represent that output from the Services was human-generated when it is not."

This goes back to the previous point about copyright. You cannot claim that you generated the output from ChatGPT, even though you provided the prompts. Therefore, you cannot claim copyright for the output.

Author's Acknowledgments

Many thanks to Jim Minatel for asking me to write this book, Lynn Northrup for editing it skillfully, Pete Gaughan for providing logistical and technical support, Straive for laying out the pages, and Evelyn Wellborn for proofreading it closely.

About the Author

Guy Hart-Davis is the author of more than 180 computer books, including *Teach Yourself VISUALLY HTML and CSS, 2nd Edition; Teach Yourself VISUALLY iPhone 14; macOS Sonoma For Dummies; Teach Yourself VISUALLY MacBook Pro and MacBook Air; Teach Yourself VISUALLY Google Workspace; Teach Yourself VISUALLY Chromebook; Teach Yourself VISUALLY Word 2019; Teach Yourself VISUALLY iPad; and Teach Yourself VISUALLY Android Phones and Tablets, 2nd Edition.*

Index